# RAISING THE COFFEE BAR

**100 Irresistible Coffeehouse-style Recipes
including Sofia's Signatures**

Content Creation: Katie Barry

Recipe Development: Euro-Pro Culinary Innovation Team

Creative Directors: Karen Bedard and Lauren Wiernasz

Design/Layout: Talia Mangeym

Photo Direction: Lauren Wiernasz, Talia Mangeym, and Jade Liu

Copywriters: Karen Bedard and Laurie Asmus

Copy Editor: Elizabeth Skladany

Photography: Michael Piazza and Quentin Bacon

Published in the United States of America by

Great Flavors LLC
P.O. Box 150
New Hope, PA 18938

ISBN: 978-1-4951-6359-3

10    9    8    7    6    5    4    3    2    1

Printed in China

# THE BEST COFFEE HOUSE IN TOWN

## IS ON YOUR COUNTERTOP.

Want rich coffee flavor? The Ninja Coffee Bar™ really brings it home, turning your favorite coffee into anything-but-basic black. Not to mention all the freshly brewed Over Ice drinks and frothy, flavorful Specialty beverages you can whip up at the touch of a button. It's practically an embarrassment of richness. In fact, don't be surprised if neighbors start lining up at your door.

# MENU

# HOT

# COLD

# SWEETS

# SOFIA'S SIGNATURES

### FAVORITE RECIPES

Look for Sofia's signature recipes and
personal tips sprinkled throughout the book. S

# SOFIA VERGARA

ACTRESS

COFFEE
LOVER

HOME
BARISTA

NINJA

# GROWING UP IN COLOMBIA,

I never had to go out of my way to find rich, smooth, balanced coffee—it's just the norm there. So, for me, the bar is very, very high. Since moving to the U.S., I've been searching for that perfect cup. And although I couldn't be prouder to have recently become a citizen, there's nothing like a so-so cup of coffee to make me miss my native country.

That's why I'm so excited to help introduce you to the Ninja Coffee Bar. I work a lot, so when I'm actually home, I love that I can invite friends over and impress them with all the different types of drinks I can whip up. A smooth, rich black coffee, a delicious flat white, a refreshing maple chicory iced coffee—you name it, I can make it. I'm happy to say that my search for the perfect cup is over. And now, so is yours.

# THE BRAINS
# BEHIND
# THE BREWS

## AUTO-iQ™
### ONE-TOUCH INTELLIGENCE

Auto-iQ™ Technology draws just the right amount of water needed from the reservoir, based on the brew size (from Cup to Travel Mug to Carafe) and brew type you select.

Only Ninja's Auto-iQ One-Touch Intelligence allows you to

# CHOOSE A SIZE,
# CHOOSE A BREW.

# THERMAL FLAVOR EXTRACTION™ TECHNOLOGY

Ninja's patent-pending brewing technology is designed to deliver better, richer-tasting coffee with variable richness levels that are never bitter. Only the Ninja Coffee Bar™ has Thermal Flavor Extraction™ Technology, which truly unlocks the full flavor potential of your coffee using automated controls for:

- Temperature Calibration
- Pre-Infusion
- Coffee Saturation

### Brew Types
This unique brewing technology knows just the right amount of flavor to extract to achieve just the strength you want.

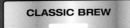

Smooth, balanced flavor from your favorite coffee.

Richer, more intense than Classic, but not bitter coffee flavor that stands up to milk, cream, or flavoring.

Specially designed to brew hot over ice to lock in flavor for a freshly brewed iced coffee that is not watered down. **Always fill your vessel with ice before brewing.**

Super-rich concentrate designed to create hot milk-based, iced, and frozen blended coffeehouse-style drinks.

# COOL OFF
# A CROWD

Make a half or full carafe of iced coffee and frozen blended drinks, and chill out with your friends. Serve up to 4 people with one brewing.

## TO EACH THEIR OWN

If a guest would like a more personalized beverage, whip up a hot, iced, or blended coffee drink just the way they like it.

DRIP STOP

NINJA

# THE CONCENTRATION CONTINUUM

The brew types on the Ninja Coffee Bar don't just indicate what types of beverages you can create, they also reflect graduated levels of coffee-to-water concentration. Starting with Classic Brew and the slightly more intense Rich Brew, dial up the concentration intensity 2x with Over Ice Brew and 3x with Specialty Brew. Each selection precisely calibrates the right flavor, richness, and strength for the beverage you want to make.

CLASSIC     RICH     OVER ICE     SPECIALTY

## CLASSIC

Smooth, rich, balanced flavor from your favorite coffee.

## RICH

Slightly more intense flavor richness than Classic Brew.

## OVER ICE

Concentration level jumps to 2x the flavor richness of Classic Brew to account for ice.

## SPECIALTY

Super-rich concentrate is about 3x the flavor richness of Classic Brew, yielding significantly less volume.

# GROUNDS FOR PERFECTION

# FRESH BEANS

For the most flavorful coffee, it's best to grind fresh whole beans right before you brew.

# MEDIUM GRIND

We suggest using a medium grind for the Ninja Coffee Bar™ and then adjusting to your liking.

# FILTERED WATER

Using fresh, filtered water is recommended for the best flavor.

# CHOOSE A SIZE

## The Scoop on Scoops

We've included this smart double-sided scoop—one side for single serve (Cup and Travel Mug) and one for carafe.

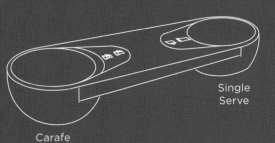

Carafe

Single Serve

| SINGLE SERVE | NINJA SCOOP Single-Serve Side | TABLESPOONS |
|---|---|---|
| CUP | 2-3 Scoops | 2-3 Tbsp. |
| TRAVEL MUG | 3-4 Scoops | 3-4 Tbsp. |

| CARAFE | NINJA SCOOP Carafe Side | TABLESPOONS |
|---|---|---|
| HALF CARAFE | 2-3 Scoops | 5-7 Tbsp. |
| FULL CARAFE | 4-6 Scoops | 8-12 Tbsp. |

# CREATE AN INSTANT CLASSIC

**Hot, rich, and smooth**

**Balanced flavor**

**Not bitter, not sour**

**TIP:**
Want your coffee to have a milder flavor? Try a coarser grind.

## PERFECT CLASSIC COFFEE

1. Add 2–3 Ninja® Single-Serve Scoops of your favorite ground coffee.
2. Add filtered water.
3. Place your cup on the single-cup platform.
4. Select the **CUP** setting.
5. Press the **CLASSIC BREW** button.

**CLASSIC BREW**

**Care to share with a friend?**
Add 4–6 Ninja Carafe scoops of your favorite ground coffee and set your carafe in place.

# STRIKE IT
# RICH

**Bolder, more intense than Classic Brew**

**Robust flavor stands up to milk, cream, and flavorings**

**Always smooth—not bitter or sour**

**TIP:**
Want hotter coffee? Before you brew into a ceramic coffee mug or the carafe, rinse it with hot water to warm it up.

DRIP STOP

## PERFECT RICH COFFEE

1. Add 2–3 Ninja® Single-Serve Scoops of your favorite ground coffee.
2. Add filtered water.
3. Place your cup on the single-cup platform.
4. Select the **CUP** setting.
5. Press the **RICH BREW** button.

**RICH BREW**

**Need to go strong all day?**
Add 4–6 Ninja Carafe scoops of your favorite ground coffee and set your carafe in place.

# BRRREW IT HOT
# OVER
# ICE

**Deep color, rich flavor— not watered down**

**Brews fresh, hot coffee over ice to lock in flavor**

**Delicious, distinctive aroma**

**TIP:**
Be sure that your cup, travel mug, or carafe is completely full of ice before brewing.

---

### PERFECT ICED COFFEE

1. Add 2–3 Ninja® Single-Serve Scoops of your favorite ground coffee.
2. Add filtered water.
3. Place a plastic cup full of ice on the single-cup platform.
4. Select the **CUP** setting.
5. Press the **OVER ICE BREW** button.

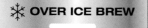

❄ **OVER ICE BREW**

**Want to please a crowd?**
Add 4-6 Ninja Carafe scoops of your favorite ground coffee and set your carafe full of ice in place.

DRIP STOP

**Important Notice: Do not use glassware.**

# CONCENTRATED COFFEE IS OUR
# SPECIALTY

**Strongest, richest flavor**

**Concentrated coffee delivers the perfect cappuccino-style coffee, latte, and flat white**

**Ideal for iced and frozen blended drinks**

**TIP:**
When choosing a size, select the Travel Cup setting for more volume and the strongest, most intense concentrated coffee.

## PERFECT CAPPUCCINO-STYLE COFFEE

1. Add 3–4 Ninja® Single-Serve Scoops of your favorite ground coffee.
2. Add filtered water.
3. Froth milk using your Ninja Easy Frother™, pour frothed milk into a mug, and place mug on the single-cup platform.
4. Select the **TRAVEL** setting.
5. Press the **SPECIALTY BREW** button.

**SPECIALTY BREW**
(CONCENTRATED COFFEE)

**Did you know?**
Our Specialty brews are small in volume, but each serving size packs a powerful punch of flavor.

In the Specialty Brew setting, the Cup size makes 3.1 ounces* of coffee concentrate, while the Travel Mug size makes 4.0 ounces.*
*approximate brew volumes

# HOT

## NINJA
### COFFEE BAR™

**Size:** Travel Mug setting
**Brew:** Classic
**Makes:** 1 (16-ounce) serving

 CLASSIC BREW

# Very Vanilla Coffee

## INGREDIENTS

4 Ninja® Single-Serve Scoops
(or 4 tablespoons) ground coffee

2 tablespoons French vanilla syrup

¼ cup half & half

## DIRECTIONS

1. Following the measurement above, place the ground coffee into the brew basket.

2. Place vanilla syrup and half & half into a mug. Microwave for 30 seconds, then set mug in place to brew.

3. Select the Travel Mug size; press the Classic Brew button.

4. When brew is complete, stir to combine.

**Size:** Travel Mug setting
**Brew:** Classic
**Makes:** 1 (16-ounce) serving

CLASSIC BREW

# Crème de Caramel Coffee

## INGREDIENTS

4 Ninja® Single-Serve Scoops (or 4 tablespoons) ground coffee

2 tablespoons caramel syrup

¼ cup half & half

## DIRECTIONS

1. Following the measurement above, place the ground coffee into the brew basket.
2. Place caramel syrup and half & half into a mug. Microwave for 30 seconds, then set mug in place to brew.
3. Select the Travel Mug size; press the Classic Brew button.
4. When brew is complete, stir to combine.

CLASSIC BREW

# Mocha Hazelnut Delight Coffee

## INGREDIENTS

3 Ninja® Single-Serve Scoops (or 3 tablespoons) ground coffee

2 tablespoons chocolate syrup

2 tablespoons hazelnut syrup

¼ cup whole milk

## DIRECTIONS

1. Following the measurement above, place the ground coffee into the brew basket.

2. Place chocolate syrup, hazelnut syrup, and milk into a mug. Microwave for 30 seconds, then set mug in place to brew.

3. Select the Cup size; press the Classic Brew button.

4. When brew is complete, stir to combine.

**CLASSIC BREW**

# Maple Pecan Coffee

## INGREDIENTS

6 Ninja® Carafe Scoops (or 12 tablespoons) ground pecan-flavored coffee

½ cup heavy cream

2 tablespoons maple syrup

½ teaspoon ground cinnamon, plus more for garnish

## DIRECTIONS

1. Following the measurement above, place the ground coffee into the brew basket.
2. Set the carafe in place to brew.
3. Select the Full Carafe size; press the Classic Brew button.
4. While coffee is brewing, whip heavy cream with maple syrup and cinnamon until soft peaks form.
5. When brew is complete, pour coffee into 4 mugs; top each with a generous dollop of whipped cream and sprinkle with cinnamon.

**Size:** Cup setting
**Brew:** Rich
**Makes:** 1 (12-ounce) serving

RICH BREW

# Too Good Toffee Coffee

## INGREDIENTS

3 Ninja® Single-Serve Scoops (or 3 tablespoons) ground coffee

1 tablespoon butterscotch or caramel sauce

1 tablespoon dark brown sugar

¼ teaspoon vanilla extract

⅛ teaspoon salt

¼ cup heavy cream

## DIRECTIONS

1. Following the measurement above, place the ground coffee into the brew basket.

2. Place butterscotch or caramel sauce, brown sugar, vanilla extract, and salt into a mug; set mug in place to brew.

3. Select the Cup size; press the Rich Brew button.

4. While coffee is brewing, place cream into the glass jar of the Ninja Easy Frother™. Microwave on High for 1 minute. Remove from microwave, secure lid, and pump the Frother 10 times. Or use a small microwave-safe jar with lid; secure lid, shake cream until foamy, remove lid, and microwave on High for 1 minute until cream is hot and froth is set.

5. When brew is complete, stir to combine, then gently pour frothed cream into coffee.

**RICH BREW**

# Café Con Chocolate ⓢ

## INGREDIENTS

3 Ninja® Carafe Scoops (or 6 tablespoons) ground coffee

2 packets hot chocolate mix

1 ½ cups whole milk, warm, divided

Whipped cream, for garnish

Chocolate syrup, for garnish

## DIRECTIONS

1. Following the measurement above, place the ground coffee into the brew basket.
2. In a measuring cup, stir together hot chocolate mix and ½ cup milk until well combined. Stir in remaining milk and mix well.
3. Pour hot chocolate mixture into the carafe; set carafe in place to brew.
4. Select the Half Carafe size; press the Rich Brew button.
5. When brew is complete, gently stir to combine and divide between 4 cups. Top with whipped cream and chocolate syrup.

**Size:** Cup setting
**Brew:** Rich
**Makes:** 1 (10-ounce) serving

RICH BREW

# Coconut Hazelnut Coffee

### INGREDIENTS

3 Ninja® Single-Serve Scoops (or 3 tablespoons) ground coconut coffee

2 tablespoons hazelnut syrup

2 tablespoons half & half

### DIRECTIONS

1. Following the measurement above, place the ground coffee into the brew basket.

2. Place hazelnut syrup and half & half into a mug; set mug in place to brew.

3. Select the Cup size; press the Rich Brew button.

4. When brew is complete, stir well to combine.

**Size:** Cup setting
**Brew:** Classic
**Makes:** 1 (12-ounce) serving

CLASSIC BREW

# Salted Caramel Coffee

### INGREDIENTS

3 Ninja® Single-Serve Scoops (or 3 tablespoons) ground coffee

2 tablespoons caramel syrup

2 tablespoons half & half

Dash sea salt

### DIRECTIONS

1. Following the measurement above, place the ground coffee into the brew basket.

2. Place caramel syrup, half & half, and salt into a mug; set mug in place to brew.

3. Select the Cup size; press the Classic Brew button.

4. When brew is complete, stir to combine.

CLASSIC BREW

# Vanilla Cinnamon Coffee

## INGREDIENTS

4 Ninja® Single-Serve Scoops (or 4 tablespoons) ground coffee

½ teaspoon ground cinnamon

3 tablespoons vanilla syrup

3 tablespoons half & half

## DIRECTIONS

1. Following the measurements above, place the ground coffee and cinnamon into the brew basket.

2. Place vanilla syrup and half & half into a mug; set mug in place to brew.

3. Select the Travel Mug size; press the Classic Brew button.

4. When brew is complete, stir to combine.

"Perfect for a subtly sweet morning drink." Sofia

**Size:** Travel Mug setting
**Brew:** Classic
**Makes:** 1 (16-ounce) serving

**CLASSIC BREW**

# Milk & Honey Coffee Ⓢ

## INGREDIENTS

4 Ninja® Single-Serve Scoops (or 4 tablespoons) ground coffee

2 tablespoons honey

¼ cup half & half

## DIRECTIONS

1. Following the measurement above, place the ground coffee into the brew basket.
2. Place honey and half & half into a mug. Microwave for 30 seconds, then set mug in place to brew.
3. Select the Travel Mug size; press the Classic Brew button.
4. When brew is complete, stir to combine.

**Size:** Cup setting
**Brew:** Classic
**Makes:** 1 (12-ounce) serving

# Creamy Blueberry Coffee

### INGREDIENTS

3 Ninja® Single-Serve Scoops (or 3 tablespoons) ground coffee

1 tablespoon blueberry tea leaves

2 tablespoons vanilla syrup

¼ cup half & half

### DIRECTIONS

1. Following the measurements above, place the ground coffee and blueberry tea leaves into the brew basket.

2. Place vanilla syrup into a mug; set mug in place to brew.

3. Select the Cup size; press the Classic Brew button.

4. While coffee is brewing, heat half & half in the microwave for 30 seconds. When brew is complete, add to coffee and stir to combine.

**Size:** Cup setting
**Brew:** Rich
**Makes:** 1 (10-ounce) serving

RICH BREW

# Chocolate Caramel Coffee

## INGREDIENTS

3 Ninja® Single-Serve Scoops (or 3 tablespoons) ground coffee

1 ½ tablespoons chocolate syrup

2 tablespoons caramel syrup

3 tablespoons half & half

## DIRECTIONS

1. Following the measurement above, place the ground coffee into the brew basket.

2. Place chocolate syrup, caramel syrup, and half & half into a mug; set mug in place to brew.

3. Select the Cup size; press the Rich Brew button.

4. When brew is complete, stir to combine.

**Size:** Travel Mug setting
**Brew:** Rich
**Makes:** 1 (14-ounce) serving

RICH BREW

# Creamy Raspberry Coffee

## INGREDIENTS

4 Ninja® Single-Serve Scoops (or 4 tablespoons) ground chocolate raspberry coffee

2 ½ tablespoons vanilla syrup

¼ cup half & half

## DIRECTIONS

1. Following the measurement above, place the ground coffee into the brew basket.

2. Place vanilla syrup and half & half into a mug; set mug in place to brew.

3. Select the Travel Mug size; press the Rich Brew button.

4. When brew is complete, stir to combine.

**Size:** Cup setting
**Brew:** Rich
**Makes:** 1 (10-ounce) serving

RICH BREW

# Caramel Nut Coffee

## INGREDIENTS

3 Ninja® Single-Serve Scoops (or 3 tablespoons) ground hazelnut coffee

2 tablespoons caramel syrup

2 tablespoons half & half

## DIRECTIONS

1. Following the measurement above, place the ground coffee into the brew basket.

2. Place caramel syrup and half & half into a mug. Microwave for 30 seconds, then set mug in place to brew.

3. Select the Cup size; press the Rich Brew button.

4. When brew is complete, stir to combine.

**Size:** Cup setting
**Brew:** Classic
**Makes:** 1 (12-ounce) serving

CLASSIC BREW

# Peppermint Vanilla Coffee

## INGREDIENTS

3 Ninja® Single-Serve Scoops (or 3 tablespoons) ground French vanilla coffee

2 ½ tablespoons vanilla syrup

1 drop peppermint extract

2 tablespoons half & half

## DIRECTIONS

1. Following the measurement above, place the ground coffee into the brew basket.

2. Place vanilla syrup, peppermint, and half & half into a mug; set mug in place to brew.

3. Select the Cup size; press the Classic Brew button.

4. When brew is complete, stir to combine.

**Size:** Half Carafe setting
**Brew:** Rich
**Makes:** 2 (9-ounce) servings

RICH BREW

# Mexican Spiced Coffee

## INGREDIENTS

3 Ninja® Carafe Scoops (or 6 tablespoons) ground coffee

1 teaspoon ground cinnamon

½ teaspoon chili powder

¼ teaspoon cayenne pepper

¼ cup heavy cream

1 tablespoon unsweetened cocoa powder

1 tablespoon confectioners' sugar

## DIRECTIONS

1. Following the measurements above; stir together the ground coffee, cinnamon, chili powder, and cayenne pepper; place into the brew basket.

2. Set the carafe in place to brew.

3. Select the Half Carafe size; press the Rich Brew button.

4. While coffee is brewing, whip heavy cream with cocoa and confectioners' sugar until soft peaks form.

5. When brew is complete, pour coffee into 2 mugs and top each with whipped cream.

**Size:** Full Carafe setting
**Brew:** Rich
**Makes:** 4 (10-ounce) servings

RICH BREW

# Cardamom & Orange Vietnamese-Style Coffee

## INGREDIENTS

6 Ninja® Carafe Scoops (or 12 tablespoons) ground coffee

¼ teaspoon ground cinnamon

½ teaspoon ground ginger

½ teaspoon ground cardamom

4 pieces fresh orange peel, pith removed

5 tablespoons sweetened condensed milk

## DIRECTIONS

1. Following the measurements above, stir together the ground coffee, cinnamon, ginger, and cardamom; place into the brew basket.

2. Place the orange peel into the carafe; set carafe in place to brew.

3. Select the Full Carafe size; press the Rich Brew button.

4. When brew is complete, gently stir in sweetened condensed milk.

RICH BREW

# Licorice Over Louisiana Coffee Ⓢ

## INGREDIENTS

3 Ninja® Single-Serve Scoops (or 3 tablespoons) ground coffee & chicory blend (found in your grocer's coffee aisle)

2 teaspoons anise seed

1 teaspoon cane sugar

½ cup 1% milk

## DIRECTIONS

1. Following the measurements above, place the ground coffee & chicory blend and anise seed into the brew basket.

2. Place sugar into a mug; set mug in place to brew.

3. Select the Cup size; press the Rich Brew button.

4. While coffee is brewing, place milk into the glass jar of the Ninja Easy Frother™. Microwave on High for 1 minute. Remove from microwave, secure lid, and pump the Frother 15 times. Or use a small microwave-safe jar with lid; secure lid, shake milk until foamy, remove lid, and microwave on High for 1 minute until milk is hot and froth is set.

5. When brew is complete, gently pour frothed milk into coffee.

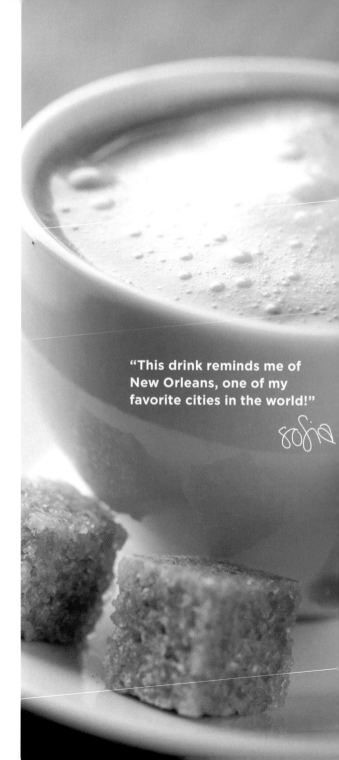

"This drink reminds me of New Orleans, one of my favorite cities in the world!"

Sofia

CLASSIC BREW

# Cinnamon Graham Latte

## INGREDIENTS

3 Ninja® Single-Serve Scoops (or 3 tablespoons) ground coffee

¼ teaspoon ground cinnamon

½ teaspoon molasses

½ teaspoon honey

¼ cup half & half

2 tablespoons marshmallow topping

1 teaspoon vanilla extract

2 teaspoons crushed cinnamon graham crackers

## DIRECTIONS

1. Following the measurement above, place the ground coffee into the brew basket.

2. Place cinnamon, molasses, and honey into a mug; set mug in place to brew.

3. Select the Cup size; press the Classic Brew button.

4. While coffee is brewing, place half & half, marshmallow topping, and vanilla extract into the glass jar of the Ninja Easy Frother™. Microwave on High for 1 minute. Remove from microwave, secure lid, and pump the Frother 10 times. Or use a small microwave-safe jar with lid; secure lid, shake half & half mixture until foamy, remove lid, and microwave on High for 1 minute until mixture is hot and froth is set.

5. When brew is complete, stir to combine, then gently pour frothed mixture into coffee. Sprinkle with crushed cinnamon graham crackers.

**Size:** Cup setting
**Brew:** Rich
**Makes:** 1 (13-ounce) serving

RICH BREW

# Lavender Luxe Coffee

## INGREDIENTS

3 Ninja® Single-Serve Scoops (or 3 tablespoons) ground coffee

1 teaspoon dried lavender, plus pinch for garnish

½ cup lowfat milk

1 tablespoon honey

## DIRECTIONS

1. Following the measurements above, stir together the ground coffee and dried lavender; place into the brew basket.

2. Set a mug in place to brew.

3. Select the Cup size; press the Rich Brew button.

4. While coffee is brewing, place milk and honey into the glass jar of the Ninja Easy Frother™. Microwave on High for 1 minute. Remove from microwave, secure lid, and pump the Frother 15 times. Or use a small microwave-safe jar with lid; secure lid, shake milk and honey until foamy, remove lid, and microwave on High for 1 minute until mixture is hot and froth is set.

5. When brew is complete, gently pour frothed mixture into coffee and sprinkle with dried lavender.

**Size:** Travel Mug setting
**Brew:** Specialty
**Makes:** 1 (12-ounce) serving

**SPECIALTY BREW**
(CONCENTRATED COFFEE)

# Cappuccino-Style Coffee

### INGREDIENTS

4 Ninja® Single-Serve Scoops (or 4 tablespoons) ground coffee

5 ounces 1% milk

### DIRECTIONS

1. Following the measurement above, place the ground coffee into the brew basket.

2. While coffee is brewing, place milk into the glass jar of the Ninja Easy Frother™. Microwave on High for 1 minute. Remove from microwave, secure lid, and pump the Frother 15 times. Or use a small microwave-safe jar with lid; secure lid, shake milk until foamy, remove lid, and microwave on High for 1 minute until milk is hot and froth is set.

3. Pour frothed milk into a mug; set mug in place to brew.

4. Select the Travel Mug size; press the Specialty Brew button.

5. When brew is complete, sweeten as desired.

**SPECIALTY BREW**
(CONCENTRATED COFFEE)

# Flat White Coffee Ⓢ

## INGREDIENTS

4 Ninja® Single-Serve Scoops (or 4 tablespoons) ground coffee

5 ounces whole milk

## DIRECTIONS

1. Following the measurement above, place the ground coffee into the brew basket.

2. Set a mug in place to brew.

3. Select the Travel Mug size; press the Specialty Brew button.

4. While coffee is brewing, place milk into the glass jar of the Ninja Easy Frother™. Microwave on High for 1 minute. Remove from microwave, secure lid, and pump the Frother 10 times. Or use a small microwave-safe jar with lid; secure lid, shake milk until foamy, remove lid, and microwave on High for 1 minute until milk is hot and froth is set.

5. When brew is complete, use a spoon to hold back the large foam from the frothed milk and allow the microfoam to pour into coffee in a steady stream. Top with a dollop of foam in the middle of the coffee.

**Size:** Cup setting
**Brew:** Specialty
**Makes:** 1 (12-ounce) serving

# Caramel Macchiato

## INGREDIENTS

3 Ninja® Single-Serve Scoops (or 3 tablespoons) ground coffee

½ cup 1% milk

2 tablespoons caramel sauce, plus more for garnish

## DIRECTIONS

1. Following the measurement above, place the ground coffee into the brew basket.

2. Set a mug in place to brew.

3. Select the Cup size, press the Specialty Brew button.

4. While coffee is brewing, place milk and caramel sauce into the glass jar of the Ninja Easy Frother™. Microwave on High for 1 minute. Remove from microwave, secure lid, and pump the Frother 15 times. Or use a small microwave-safe jar with lid; secure lid, shake milk and caramel sauce until foamy, remove lid, and microwave on High for 1 minute until mixture is hot and froth is set.

5. When brew is complete, gently pour frothed mixture into coffee. Drizzle with additional caramel sauce.

# Mocha Latte

## INGREDIENTS

4 Ninja® Single-Serve Scoops (or 4 tablespoons) ground coffee

1 tablespoon chocolate syrup

½ cup 1% milk

## DIRECTIONS

1. Following the measurement above, place the ground coffee into the brew basket.

2. Place chocolate syrup into a mug; set mug in place to brew.

3. Select the Travel Mug size; press the Specialty Brew button.

4. While coffee is brewing, place milk into the glass jar of the Ninja Easy Frother™. Microwave on High for 1 minute. Remove from microwave, secure lid, and pump the Frother 15 times. Or use a small microwave-safe jar with lid; secure lid, shake milk until foamy, remove lid, and microwave on High for 1 minute until milk is hot and froth is set.

5. When brew is complete, stir to combine, then gently pour frothed milk into coffee.

**Size:** Travel Mug setting
**Brew:** Specialty
**Makes:** 1 (10-ounce) serving

**SPECIALTY BREW**
(CONCENTRATED COFFEE)

# Vanilla Latte

## INGREDIENTS

4 Ninja® Single-Serve Scoops (or 4 tablespoons) ground coffee

2 tablespoons vanilla syrup

½ cup 1% milk

## DIRECTIONS

1. Following the measurement above, place the ground coffee into the brew basket.

2. Place vanilla syrup into a mug; set mug in place to brew.

3. Select the Travel Mug size; press the Specialty Brew button.

4. While coffee is brewing, place milk into the glass jar of the Ninja Easy Frother™. Microwave on High for 1 minute. Remove from microwave, secure lid, and pump the Frother 15 times. Or use a small microwave-safe jar with lid; secure lid, shake milk until foamy, remove lid, and microwave on High for 1 minute until milk is hot and froth is set.

5. When brew is complete, stir to combine, then gently pour frothed milk into coffee.

# Café au Lait

## INGREDIENTS

3 Ninja® Single-Serve Scoops (or 3 tablespoons) ground coffee

½ cup 1% milk

## DIRECTIONS

1. Following the measurement above, place the ground coffee into the brew basket.

2. Place milk into a mug; set mug in place to brew.

3. Select the Travel Mug size; press the Specialty Brew Button.

4. When brew is complete, stir to combine.

**Size:** Cup setting
**Brew:** Specialty
**Makes:** 1 (7-ounce) serving

**SPECIALTY BREW**
(CONCENTRATED COFFEE)

# Café Americano

## INGREDIENTS

3 Ninja® Single-Serve Scoops (or 3 tablespoons) ground coffee

½ cup hot water

Milk and sugar to taste, if desired

## DIRECTIONS

1. Following the measurement above, place the ground coffee into the brew basket.
2. Set a mug in place to brew.
3. Select the Cup size; press the Specialty Brew button.
4. When brew is complete, stir in hot water. Add milk and sugar to taste, if desired.

**Want a stronger flavor?**
Use 4 Ninja Single-Serve Scoops (or 4 tablespoons) ground coffee, select the Travel Mug setting, and stir in the same amount of hot water.

**Size:** Cup setting
**Brew:** Specialty
**Makes:** 1 (12-ounce) serving

**SPECIALTY BREW**
(CONCENTRATED COFFEE)

# Pumpkin Spice Latte

## INGREDIENTS

3 Ninja® Single-Serve Scoops (or 3 tablespoons) ground coffee

½ cup whole milk

1 tablespoon dark brown sugar

¼ teaspoon pumpkin pie spice, plus more for garnish

Pinch salt

## DIRECTIONS

1. Following the measurement above, place the ground coffee into the brew basket.

2. Set a mug in place to brew.

3. Select the Cup size; press the Specialty Brew button.

4. While coffee is brewing, place remaining ingredients in the glass jar of the Ninja Easy Frother™. Microwave on High for 1 minute. Remove from microwave, secure lid, and pump the Frother 15 times. Or use a small microwave-safe jar with lid; secure lid, shake milk mixture until foamy, remove lid, and microwave on High for 1 minute until mixture is hot and froth is set.

5. When brew is complete, gently pour frothed mixture over brewed coffee. Sprinkle with pumpkin pie spice.

**SPECIALTY BREW**
(CONCENTRATED COFFEE)

# Marshmallow Mint Latte ⓢ

## INGREDIENTS

3 Ninja® Single-Serve Scoops (or 3 tablespoons) ground coffee

3 squares chocolate-mint sandwich candy, chopped, plus more for garnish

½ cup 1% milk

¼ cup marshmallow cream

## DIRECTIONS

1. Following the measurement above, place the ground coffee into the brew basket.

2. Place chopped chocolate-mint candy into a mug; set mug in place to brew.

3. Select the Cup size; press the Specialty Brew button.

4. While coffee is brewing, place milk and marshmallow cream into the glass jar of the Ninja Easy Frother™. Microwave on High for 1 minute. Remove from microwave, secure lid, and pump the Frother 10 times. Or use a small microwave-safe jar with lid; secure lid, shake milk and marshmallow cream until foamy, remove lid, and microwave on High for 1 minute until mixture is hot and froth is set.

5. When brew is complete, gently pour frothed mixture into coffee and garnish with additional chopped chocolate-mint candy.

"Everyone knows I love desserts, and this recipe is just perfect."

*Sofia*

**Size:** Travel Mug setting
**Brew:** Specialty
**Makes:** 1 (10-ounce) serving

**SPECIALTY BREW**
(CONCENTRATED COFFEE)

# White Chocolate Hazelnut Latte

## INGREDIENTS

4 Ninja® Single-Serve Scoops (or 4 tablespoons) ground hazelnut coffee

2 tablespoons white chocolate syrup, plus more for garnish

½ cup 1% milk

## DIRECTIONS

1. Following the measurement above, place the ground coffee into the brew basket.

2. Place white chocolate syrup into a mug; set mug in place to brew.

3. Select the Travel Mug size; press the Specialty Brew button.

4. While coffee is brewing, place milk into the glass jar of the Ninja Easy Frother™. Microwave on High for 1 minute. Remove from microwave, secure lid, and pump the Frother 15 times. Or use a small microwave-safe jar with lid; secure lid, shake milk until foamy, remove lid, and microwave on High for 1 minute until milk is hot and froth is set.

5. When brew is complete, stir to combine, then gently pour frothed milk into coffee. Drizzle with additional white chocolate syrup.

**SPECIALTY BREW**
(CONCENTRATED COFFEE)

# Cinnamon Mocha Latte

## INGREDIENTS

4 Ninja® Single-Serve Scoops (or 4 tablespoons) ground coffee

½ teaspoon ground cinnamon, plus more for garnish.

2 tablespoons chocolate syrup

½ cup 1% milk

## DIRECTIONS

1. Following the measurements above, place the ground coffee and cinnamon into the brew basket.

2. Place chocolate syrup into a mug; set mug in place to brew.

3. Select the Travel Mug size; press the Specialty Brew button.

4. While coffee is brewing, place milk into the glass jar of the Ninja Easy Frother™. Microwave on High for 1 minute. Remove from microwave, secure lid, and pump the Frother 15 times. Or use a small microwave-safe jar with lid; secure lid, shake milk until foamy, remove lid, and microwave on High for 1 minute until milk is hot and froth is set.

5. When brew is complete, stir to combine, then gently pour frothed milk into coffee. Sprinkle with additional cinnamon.

**Size:** Travel Mug setting
**Brew:** Specialty
**Makes:** 1 (10-ounce) serving

SPECIALTY BREW
(CONCENTRATED COFFEE)

# Caramel Nutmeg Latte

## INGREDIENTS

4 Ninja® Single-Serve Scoops (or 4 tablespoons) ground coffee

½ teaspoon ground nutmeg, plus more for garnish

2 tablespoons caramel syrup

½ cup 1% milk

## DIRECTIONS

1. Following the measurements above, place the ground coffee and nutmeg into the brew basket.

2. Place caramel syrup into a mug; set mug in place to brew.

3. Select the Travel Mug size; press the Specialty Brew button.

4. While coffee is brewing, place milk into the glass jar of the Ninja Easy Frother™. Microwave on High for 1 minute. Remove from microwave, secure lid, and pump the Frother 15 times. Or use a small microwave-safe jar with lid; secure lid, shake milk until foamy, remove lid, and microwave on High for 1 minute until milk is hot and froth is set.

5. When brew is complete, stir to combine, then gently pour frothed milk into coffee. Sprinkle with additional nutmeg.

**Size:** Travel Mug setting
**Brew:** Specialty
**Makes:** 1 (10-ounce) serving

SPECIALTY BREW
(CONCENTRATED COFFEE)

# Cardamom Vanilla Latte

## INGREDIENTS

4 Ninja® Single-Serve Scoops (or 4 tablespoons) ground French vanilla coffee

1/2 teaspoon ground cardamom

2 tablespoons vanilla syrup

1/2 cup 1% milk

## DIRECTIONS

1. Following the measurements above, place the ground coffee and cardamom into the brew basket.

2. Place vanilla syrup into a mug; set mug in place to brew.

3. Select the Travel Mug size; press the Specialty Brew button.

4. While coffee is brewing, place milk into the glass jar of the Ninja Easy Frother™. Microwave on High for 1 minute. Remove from microwave, secure lid, and pump the Frother 15 times. Or use a small microwave-safe jar with lid; secure lid, shake milk until foamy, remove lid, and microwave on High for 1 minute until milk is hot and froth is set.

5. When brew is complete, stir to combine, then gently pour frothed milk into coffee.

"Using coconut milk in a latte is such an easy way to change up your drink."

*Sofia*

**Size:** Travel Mug setting
**Brew:** Specialty
**Makes:** 1 (10-ounce) serving

**SPECIALTY BREW**
(CONCENTRATED COFFEE)

# Coconut Milk Latte Ⓢ

## INGREDIENTS

4 Ninja® Single-Serve Scoops (or 4 tablespoons) ground coffee

2 tablespoons vanilla syrup

½ cup coconut milk beverage

## DIRECTIONS

1. Following the measurement above, place the ground coffee into the brew basket.
2. Place vanilla syrup into a mug; set mug in place to brew.
3. Select the Travel Mug size; press the Specialty Brew button.
4. While coffee is brewing, place coconut milk into the glass jar of the Ninja Easy Frother™. Microwave on High for 1 minute. Remove from microwave, secure lid, and pump the Frother 15 times. Or use a small microwave-safe jar with lid; secure lid, shake coconut milk until foamy, remove lid, and microwave on High for 1 minute until milk is hot and froth is set.
5. When brew is complete, stir to combine, then gently pour frothed coconut milk into coffee.

**SPECIALTY BREW**
(CONCENTRATED COFFEE)

# Silk Road Coffee

## INGREDIENTS

3 Ninja® Single-Serve Scoops (or 3 tablespoons) ground coffee

$3/4$ teaspoon ground ginger

$3/4$ teaspoon ground cinnamon

$1/2$ teaspoon ground cardamom

$1/4$ teaspoon ground nutmeg

$1/4$ teaspoon ground black pepper

$1/8$ teaspoon ground cloves

$1/2$ cup 2% milk

1 tablespoon French vanilla syrup

Cracked black pepper, for garnish

## DIRECTIONS

1. Following the measurements above, stir together the ground coffee and spices; place into the brew basket.

2. Set a mug in place to brew.

3. Select the Cup size; press the Specialty Brew button.

4. While coffee is brewing, place milk and vanilla syrup into the glass jar of the Ninja Easy Frother™. Microwave on High for 1 minute. Remove from microwave, secure lid, and pump the Frother 15 times. Or use a small microwave-safe jar with lid; secure lid, shake milk and vanilla syrup until foamy, remove lid, and microwave on High for 1 minute until mixture is hot and froth is set.

5. When brew is complete, gently pour frothed mixture into coffee and sprinkle with cracked black pepper.

**SPECIALTY BREW**
(CONCENTRATED COFFEE)

# Irish Coffee

## INGREDIENTS

3 Ninja® Single-Serve Scoops (or 3 tablespoons) ground coffee

2 teaspoons brown sugar, divided

½ cup heavy cream

1 teaspoon + 3 tablespoons Irish whiskey, divided

## DIRECTIONS

1. Following the measurement above, place the ground coffee into the brew basket.

2. Place 1 teaspoon brown sugar into a large mug; set mug in place to brew.

3. Select the Cup size; press the Specialty Brew button.

4. While coffee is brewing, whip heavy cream with 1 teaspoon brown sugar and 1 teaspoon Irish whiskey until soft peaks form.

5. When brew is complete, add remaining whiskey and stir to combine. Divide between 2 cups and top with whipped cream.

# Bourbon-Spiked Pumpkin Latte

## INGREDIENTS

3 Ninja® Single-Serve Scoops (or 3 tablespoons) ground coffee

3 tablespoons (1.5-ounce shot) bourbon

1/4 teaspoon vanilla extract

1 tablespoon packed dark brown sugar

Pinch salt

1/4 teaspoon pumpkin pie spice, plus more for garnish

1/2 cup 1% milk

## DIRECTIONS

1. Following the measurement above, place the ground coffee into the brew basket.

2. Place remaining ingredients, except milk, into a large mug; set mug in place to brew.

3. Select the Cup size; press the Specialty Brew button.

4. While coffee is brewing, place milk into the glass jar of the Ninja Easy Frother™. Microwave on High for 1 minute. Remove from microwave, secure lid, and pump the Frother 15 times. Or use a small microwave-safe jar with lid; secure lid, shake milk until foamy, remove lid, and microwave on High for 1 minute until milk is hot and froth is set.

5. When brew is complete, stir to combine, then gently pour frothed mixture into coffee. Sprinkle with additional pumpkin pie spice.

RICH BREW

# Café Brulôt

## INGREDIENTS

3 Ninja® Carafe Scoops (or 6 tablespoons) ground coffee

2 tablespoons granulated sugar

¼ cup (2 ounces) brandy or cognac

Peel of one orange, pith removed

2 whole cloves

1 cinnamon stick

Whipped cream, for garnish

## DIRECTIONS

1. Following the measurement above, place the ground coffee into the brew basket.

2. Set the carafe in place to brew.

3. Select the Half Carafe size; press the Rich Brew button.

4. While coffee is brewing, combine sugar, brandy, orange peel, cloves, and cinnamon stick in a small saucepan; heat over low heat, stirring, until sugar dissolves. Remove and discard orange peel and spices.

5. When brew is complete, divide coffee along with brandy mixture between 4 mugs. Top each serving with whipped cream.

# CO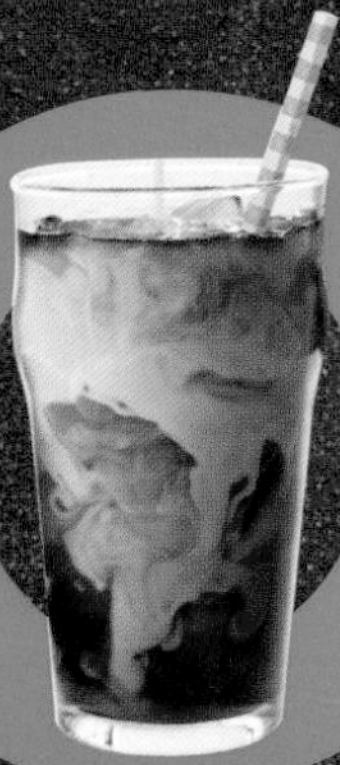LD

NINJA
COFFEE BAR™

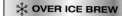 ❄ **OVER ICE BREW**

# French Vanilla Iced Coffee

## INGREDIENTS

3 Ninja® Single-Serve Scoops (or 3 tablespoons) ground coffee

2 cups ice

2 tablespoons French vanilla syrup

¼ cup half & half

## DIRECTIONS

1. Following the measurement above, place the ground coffee into the brew basket.

2. Place the ice, vanilla syrup, and half & half into a large plastic cup; set cup in place to brew.

3. Select the Cup size; press the Over Ice Brew button.

4. When brew is complete, stir to combine.

**Want it a little milder?**
Use 2 Ninja Single-Serve Scoops instead of 3.

**Size:** Travel Mug setting
**Brew:** Over Ice
**Makes:** 1 (18-ounce) serving

❄ **OVER ICE BREW**

# Hazelnut Iced Coffee

## INGREDIENTS

4 Ninja® Single-Serve Scoops (or 4 tablespoons)
ground coffee

2 cups ice

3 tablespoons hazelnut syrup

½ cup half & half

## DIRECTIONS

1. Following the measurement above, place the
   ground coffee into the brew basket.

2. Place the ice, hazelnut syrup, and half & half into
   a large plastic cup; set cup in place to brew.

3. Select the Travel Mug size; press the Over Ice
   Brew button.

4. When brew is complete, stir to combine.

**Want it a little sweeter?**
Add more hazelnut syrup.

❄ **OVER ICE BREW**

# Thai-Style Iced Coffee Ⓢ

## INGREDIENTS

3 Ninja® Single-Serve Scoops (or 3 tablespoons) ground coffee

¼ cup sweetened condensed milk

¼ cup 2% milk

2 cups ice

## DIRECTIONS

1. Following the measurement above, place the ground coffee into the brew basket.

2. Place sweetened condensed milk and 2% milk into a large plastic cup; stir to combine. Add the ice to the cup; set cup in place to brew.

3. Select the Cup size; press the Over Ice Brew button.

4. When brew is complete, stir to combine.

"The condensed milk gives this drink a sweet creamy flavor, perfect for a Summer day."

Sofie

"The chicory is the reason this is one of my favorite drinks."

*Sofia*

**Size:** Cup setting
**Brew:** Over Ice
**Makes:** 1 (18-ounce) serving

❄ OVER ICE BREW

# Maple Chicory Iced Coffee Ⓢ

### INGREDIENTS

3 Ninja® Single-Serve Scoops (or 3 tablespoons) ground coffee & chicory blend (found in your grocer's coffee aisle)

2 cups ice

¾ cup 2% milk

2 teaspoons maple syrup

### DIRECTIONS

1. Following the measurement above, place the ground coffee & chicory blend into the brew basket.
2. Place the ice, milk, and maple syrup into a large plastic cup; set cup in place to brew.
3. Select the Cup size; press the Over Ice Brew button.
4. When brew is complete, stir to combine.

**Size:** Cup setting
**Brew:** Over Ice
**Makes:** 1 (16-ounce) serving

# Mocha Mint Cooler

## INGREDIENTS

3 Ninja® Single-Serve Scoops (or 3 tablespoons) ground coffee

⅛ teaspoon peppermint extract

2 cups ice

2 tablespoons chocolate syrup

½ cup 2% milk

## DIRECTIONS

1. Following the measurements above, place the ground coffee into the brew basket and top with peppermint extract.

2. Place the ice, chocolate syrup, and milk into a large plastic cup; set cup in place to brew.

3. Select the Cup size; press the Over Ice Brew button.

4. When brew is complete, stir to combine.

❄ **OVER ICE BREW**

# Cinnamon Caramel Iced Coffee ⓢ

## INGREDIENTS

4 Ninja® Single-Serve Scoops (or 4 tablespoons) ground coffee

½ teaspoon ground cinnamon

2 cups ice

2 tablespoons half & half

2 tablespoons caramel syrup

## DIRECTIONS

1. Following the measurements above, place the ground coffee and cinnamon into the brew basket.

2. Place the ice, half & half, and caramel syrup into a large plastic cup; set cup in place to brew.

3. Select the Travel Mug size; press the Over Ice Brew button.

4. When brew is complete, stir to combine.

"Cinnamon, caramel, and coffee together? You can't go wrong!"

Sofia

**Size:** Cup setting
**Brew:** Over Ice
**Makes:** 1 (14-ounce) serving

# Coconut Caramel Iced Coffee

## INGREDIENTS

3 Ninja® Single-Serve Scoops (or 3 tablespoons) ground coconut coffee

2 cups ice

2 tablespoons caramel sauce

¼ cup half & half

## DIRECTIONS

1. Following the measurement above, place the ground coffee into the brew basket.
2. Place the ice, caramel sauce, and half & half into a large plastic cup; set cup in place to brew.
3. Select the Cup size; press the Over Ice Brew button.
4. When brew is complete, stir to combine.

**Size:** Travel Mug setting
**Brew:** Over Ice
**Makes:** 1 (16-ounce) serving

# Chocolate Raspberry Iced Coffee

## INGREDIENTS

4 Ninja® Single-Serve Scoops (or 4 tablespoons) ground chocolate raspberry coffee

2 cups ice

4 tablespoons half & half

2 tablespoons chocolate syrup

## DIRECTIONS

1. Following the measurement above, place the ground coffee into the brew basket.
2. Place the ice, half & half, and chocolate syrup into a large plastic cup; set cup in place to brew.
3. Select the Travel Mug size; press the Over Ice Brew button.
4. When brew is complete, stir to combine.

**Size:** Travel Mug setting
**Brew:** Over Ice
**Makes:** 1 (16-ounce) serving

# Pecan Caramel Iced Coffee

## INGREDIENTS

4 Ninja® Single-Serve Scoops (or 4 tablespoons) ground pecan coffee

2 cups ice

2 tablespoons half & half

2 tablespoons caramel syrup

## DIRECTIONS

1. Following the measurement above, place the ground coffee into the brew basket.

2. Place the ice, half & half, and caramel syrup into a large plastic cup; set cup in place to brew.

3. Select the Travel Mug size; press the Over Ice Brew button.

4. When brew is complete, stir to combine.

**Size:** Travel Mug setting
**Brew:** Over Ice
**Makes:** 1 (16-ounce) serving

**OUR CUPS MEASURE UP.**
The Ninja Hot & Cold Insulated Tumbler has 2-oz. measurement ribs for quick and easy recipe making.

# Creamy Caramel Iced Coffee

## INGREDIENTS

4 Ninja® Single-Serve Scoops (or 4 tablespoons) ground French vanilla coffee

2 cups ice

2 tablespoons half & half

1 tablespoon caramel syrup

1 tablespoon vanilla syrup

## DIRECTIONS

1. Following the measurement above, place the ground coffee into the brew basket.

2. Place the ice, half & half, caramel syrup, and vanilla syrup into a large plastic cup; set cup in place to brew.

3. Select the Travel Mug size; press the Over Ice Brew button.

4. When brew is complete, stir to combine.

**Size:** Travel Mug setting
**Brew:** Over Ice
**Makes:** 1 (16-ounce) serving

# Blueberries & Cream Iced Coffee

### INGREDIENTS

4 Ninja® Single-Serve Scoops (or 4 tablespoons) ground blueberry coffee

2 cups ice

2 tablespoons half & half

2 tablespoons vanilla syrup

### DIRECTIONS:

1. Following the measurement above, place the ground coffee into the brew basket.
2. Place the ice, half & half, and vanilla syrup into a large plastic cup; set cup in place to brew.
3. Select the Travel Mug size; press the Over Ice Brew button.
4. When brew is complete, stir to combine.

**Size:** Travel Mug setting
**Brew:** Over Ice
**Makes:** 1 (16-ounce) serving

# White Chocolate Hazelnut Iced Coffee

### INGREDIENTS

4 Ninja® Single-Serve Scoops (or 4 tablespoons) ground hazelnut coffee

2 cups ice

2 tablespoons half & half

2 tablespoons white chocolate syrup

### DIRECTIONS

1. Following the measurement above, place the ground coffee into the brew basket.
2. Place the ice, half & half, and white chocolate syrup into a large plastic cup; set cup in place to brew.
3. Select the Travel Mug size; press the Over Ice Brew button.
4. When brew is complete, stir to combine.

❄ OVER ICE BREW

# Gingersnap Iced Coffee

## INGREDIENTS

4 Ninja® Single-Serve Scoops (or 4 tablespoons) ground coffee

½ teaspoon ground cinnamon

¼ teaspoon ground ginger

2 cups ice

2 tablespoons half & half

2 tablespoons vanilla syrup

## DIRECTIONS

1. Following the measurements above, place the ground coffee, cinnamon, and ginger into the brew basket.

2. Place the ice, half & half, and vanilla syrup into a large plastic cup; set cup in place to brew.

3. Select the Travel Mug size; press the Over Ice Brew button.

4. When brew is complete, stir to combine.

SPECIALTY BREW
(CONCENTRATED COFFEE)

**OUR CUPS MEASURE UP.**
The Ninja Hot & Cold Insulated Tumbler has 2-oz. measurement ribs for quick and easy recipe making.

# Chocolate Caramel Nut Iced Coffee

## INGREDIENTS

4 Ninja® Single-Serve Scoops (or 4 tablespoons) ground pecan coffee

2 cups ice

2 tablespoons half & half

1 tablespoon chocolate syrup

1 tablespoon caramel syrup

## DIRECTIONS

1. Following the measurement above, place the ground coffee into the brew basket.

2. Place the ice, half & half, chocolate syrup, and caramel syrup into a large plastic cup; set cup in place to brew.

3. Select the Travel Mug size; press the Specialty Brew button.

4. When brew is complete, stir to combine.

**Size:** Cup setting
**Brew:** Over Ice
**Makes:** 1 (12-ounce) serving

❄ OVER ICE BREW

# Coffee Soda Float

## INGREDIENTS

### Coffee Soda Concentrate:

3 Ninja® Single-Serve Scoops (or 3 tablespoons) ground coffee

½ cup granulated sugar

### Float:

¼ cup coffee soda concentrate (recipe below)

½ cup vanilla ice cream

¾ cup seltzer water

## DIRECTIONS

1. Following the measurement above, place the ground coffee into the brew basket.

2. Set a mug in place to brew.

3. Select the Cup size; press the Over Ice Brew button.

4. When brew is complete, create the coffee soda concentrate by combining the brewed coffee with the sugar in a pan and cooking over high heat until sugar is dissolved, about 3 minutes. Allow to cool.

5. Pour the cooled coffee soda concentrate into a large plastic cup. Add vanilla ice cream, then carefully add seltzer water.

**Size:** Travel Mug setting
**Brew:** Specialty
**Makes:** 2 (10-ounce) servings

**SPECIALTY BREW**
(CONCENTRATED COFFEE)

# Classic Ninjaccino

## INGREDIENTS

4 Ninja® Single-Serve Scoops (or 4 tablespoons) ground coffee

3 cups ice

1/4 cup 1% milk

1/4 cup sweetened condensed milk

## DIRECTIONS

1. Following the measurement above, place the ground coffee into the brew basket.

2. Place the ice into a large plastic cup; set cup in place to brew.

3. Select the Travel Mug size; press the Specialty Brew button.

4. When brew is complete, combine coffee and ice with milk and sweetened condensed milk in a 24-ounce or larger blender container.

5. Blend until smooth, about 25 seconds; divide between 2 glasses.

**Size:** Travel Mug setting
**Brew:** Specialty
**Makes:** 2 (10-ounce) servings

**SPECIALTY BREW**
(CONCENTRATED COFFEE)

# Mocha Ninjaccino

## INGREDIENTS

4 Ninja® Single-Serve Scoops (or 4 tablespoons)
ground coffee

3 cups ice

¼ cup 1% milk

¼ cup chocolate syrup, plus more for garnish

Whipped cream, for garnish

## DIRECTIONS

1. Following the measurement above, place the ground coffee into the brew basket.

2. Place the ice into a large plastic cup; set cup in place to brew.

3. Select the Travel Mug size; press the Specialty Brew button.

4. When brew is complete, combine coffee and ice with milk and chocolate syrup in a 24-ounce or larger blender container.

5. Blend until smooth, about 25 seconds. Divide between 2 glasses, top with whipped cream, and drizzle with additional chocolate syrup.

**Want it a little sweeter?**
Add more chocolate syrup.

**SPECIALTY BREW**
(CONCENTRATED COFFEE)

# Sweet Sofiaccino Ⓢ

## INGREDIENTS

4 Ninja® Single-Serve Scoops (or 4 tablespoons) ground Colombian coffee

3 cups ice

¼ cup evaporated milk

½ cup sweetened condensed milk

Whipped cream, for garnish

Ground cinnamon, for garnish

## DIRECTIONS

1. Following the measurement above, place the ground coffee into the brew basket.

2. Place the ice into a large plastic cup; set cup in place to brew.

3. Select the Travel Mug size; press the Specialty Brew button.

4. When brew is complete, combine coffee and ice with evaporated milk and sweetened condensed milk in a 24-ounce or larger blender container.

5. Blend until smooth, about 25 seconds; divide between 2 glasses and garnish with whipped cream and cinnamon.

**"You know this drink is my favorite if I put my name on it!"**

*Sofia*

**Size:** Travel Mug setting
**Brew:** Specialty
**Makes:** 2 (12-ounce) servings

SPECIALTY BREW
(CONCENTRATED COFFEE)

# Coco-Mocho Crunch Ninjaccino

## INGREDIENTS

4 Ninja® Single-Serve Scoops (or 4 tablespoons) ground coffee

3 cups ice

½ cup lowfat milk

¼ cup chocolate syrup

3 tablespoons toasted coconut, divided

Whipped cream, for garnish

## DIRECTIONS

1. Following the measurement above, place the ground coffee into the brew basket.

2. Place the ice into a large plastic cup; set cup in place to brew.

3. Select the Travel Mug size; press the Specialty Brew button.

4. When brew is complete, combine coffee and ice with milk, chocolate syrup, and 2 tablespoons toasted coconut in a 24-ounce or larger blender container.

5. Blend until smooth, about 25 seconds; divide between 2 glasses.

6. Top with whipped cream and sprinkle with remaining tablespoon coconut.

**SPECIALTY BREW**
(CONCENTRATED COFFEE)

# Pecan Praline Ninjaccino

## INGREDIENTS

4 Ninja® Single-Serve Scoops (or 4 tablespoons) ground coffee

3 cups ice

¼ cup toasted pecans

¼ cup 1% milk

2 tablespoons butterscotch or caramel sauce

2 tablespoons packed dark brown sugar

¼ teaspoon vanilla extract

## DIRECTIONS

1. Following the measurement above, place the ground coffee into the brew basket.

2. Place the ice into a large plastic cup; set cup in place to brew.

3. Select the Travel Mug size; press the Specialty Brew button.

4. When brew is complete, combine coffee and ice with remaining ingredients in a 24-ounce or larger blender container.

5. Blend until smooth, about 25 seconds; divide between 2 glasses.

**Size:** Travel Mug setting
**Brew:** Specialty
**Makes:** 2 (10-ounce) servings

SPECIALTY BREW
(CONCENTRATED COFFEE)

# Coffee & Cream Milkshake

## INGREDIENTS

4 Ninja® Single-Serve Scoops (or 4 tablespoons) ground coffee

½ cup ice

2 cups vanilla ice cream

## DIRECTIONS

1. Following the measurement above, place the ground coffee into the brew basket.

2. Place the ice into a large plastic cup; set cup in place to brew.

3. Select the Travel Mug size; press the Specialty Brew button.

4. When brew is complete, combine coffee and ice with ice cream in a 24-ounce or larger blender container.

5. Blend until smooth, about 25 seconds; divide between 2 glasses.

**Size:** Cup setting
**Brew:** Specialty
**Makes:** 2 (8-ounce) servings

**SPECIALTY BREW**
(CONCENTRATED COFFEE)

# Coffee, Cookies & Cream Frappe

## INGREDIENTS

3 Ninja® Single-Serve Scoops (or 3 tablespoons) ground coffee

2 cups ice

½ cup coffee ice cream

4 chocolate sandwich cookies, plus 1 chopped for garnish

¼ cup milk

Whipped cream, for garnish

## DIRECTIONS

1. Following the measurement above, place the ground coffee into the brew basket.

2. Place the ice into a large plastic cup; set cup in place to brew.

3. Select the Cup size; press the Specialty Brew button.

4. When brew is complete, combine coffee and ice with ice cream, cookies, and milk in a 24-ounce or larger blender container.

5. Blend until smooth, about 25 seconds. Divide between 2 glasses; top with whipped cream and chopped cookie.

**Size:** Travel Mug setting
**Brew:** Specialty
**Makes:** 2 (12-ounce) servings

**SPECIALTY BREW**
(CONCENTRATED COFFEE)

# Caramel Ninjaccino

## INGREDIENTS

4 Ninja® Single-Serve Scoops (or 4 tablespoons) ground coffee

3 cups ice

¼ cup 1% milk

¼ cup caramel syrup

## DIRECTIONS

1. Following the measurement above, place the ground coffee into the brew basket.

2. Place the ice into a large plastic cup; set cup in place to brew.

3. Select the Travel Mug size; press the Specialty Brew button.

4. When brew is complete, combine coffee and ice with milk and caramel syrup in a 24-ounce or larger blender container.

5. Blend until smooth, about 25 seconds; divide between 2 glasses.

"This is the coffee drink that makes you feel like you are on an island."

sofia

**Size:** Travel Mug setting
**Brew:** Specialty
**Makes:** 2 (12-ounce) servings

**SPECIALTY BREW**
(CONCENTRATED COFFEE)

# Creamy Dreamy
# Vanilla Coconut Ninjaccino S

## INGREDIENTS

4 Ninja® Single-Serve Scoops (or 4 tablespoons) ground coffee

3 cups ice

⅓ cup sweetened cream of coconut

¼ cup lowfat milk

1 teaspoon vanilla extract

¼ cup toasted shredded coconut, divided

Whipped cream, for garnish

## DIRECTIONS

1. Following the measurement above, place the ground coffee into the brew basket.

2. Place the ice into a large plastic cup; set cup in place to brew.

3. Select the Travel Mug size; press the Specialty Brew button.

4. When brew is complete, combine coffee and ice with cream of coconut, milk, and vanilla in a 24-ounce or larger blender container.

6. Blend until smooth, about 25 seconds. Stir in all but 1 teaspoon shredded coconut. Divide between 2 glasses.

7. Top with whipped cream and sprinkle with remaining 1 teaspoon shredded coconut.

"This drink reminds me of my childhood by combining two of my favorite things—coffee and dulce de leche."

*Sofia*

**Size:** Travel Mug setting
**Brew:** Specialty
**Makes:** 2 (10-ounce) servings

**SPECIALTY BREW**
(CONCENTRATED COFFEE)

# Cinnamon Dulce Ninjaccino **S**

## INGREDIENTS

4 Ninja® Single-Serve Scoops (or 4 tablespoons) ground coffee

½ teaspoon ground cinnamon, plus more for garnish

3 cups ice

¼ cup whole milk

½ cup dulce de leche

Whipped cream, for garnish

## DIRECTIONS

1. Following the measurements above, place the ground coffee and cinnamon into the brew basket.

2. Place the ice into a large plastic cup; set cup in place to brew.

3. Select the Travel Mug size; press the Specialty Brew button.

4. When brew is complete, combine coffee and ice with milk and dulce de leche in a 24-ounce or larger blender container.

5. Blend until smooth, about 25 seconds; divide between 2 glasses and top with whipped cream and cinnamon

**Size:** Travel Mug setting
**Brew:** Specialty
**Makes:** 1 (12-ounce) serving

**SPECIALTY BREW**
(CONCENTRATED COFFEE)

# Iced Americano

## INGREDIENTS

4 Ninja® Single-Serve Scoops (or 4 tablespoons) ground coffee

2 cups ice

½ cup cold water, plus more if desired

Milk and sugar, to taste

## DIRECTIONS

1. Following the measurement above, place the ground coffee into the brew basket.
2. Place the ice into a large plastic cup; set cup in place to brew.
3. Select the Travel Mug size; press the Specialty Brew button.
4. When brew is complete, stir in the cold water; add milk and sugar to taste.

**Size:** Cup setting
**Brew:** Specialty
**Makes:** 1 (16-ounce) serving

# Iced Vanilla Latte

## INGREDIENTS

3 Ninja® Single-Serve Scoops (or 3 tablespoons) ground coffee

2 cups ice

2 tablespoons vanilla syrup

¾ cup whole milk

## DIRECTIONS

1. Following the measurement above, place the ground coffee into the brew basket.
2. Place the ice, vanilla syrup, and milk into a large plastic cup; set cup in place to brew.
3. Select the Cup size; press the Specialty Brew button.
4. When brew is complete, stir to combine.

**OUR CUPS MEASURE UP.**
The Ninja Hot & Cold Insulated Tumbler has 2-oz. measurement ribs for quick and easy recipe making.

**Size:** Cup setting
**Brew:** Specialty
**Makes:** 1 (16-ounce) serving

# Iced Mocha Latte

## INGREDIENTS

3 Ninja® Single-Serve Scoops (or 3 tablespoons) ground coffee

2 cups ice

2 tablespoons chocolate syrup

¾ cup whole milk

## DIRECTIONS

1. Following the measurement above, place the ground coffee into the brew basket.
2. Place the ice, chocolate syrup, and milk into a large plastic cup; set cup in place to brew.
3. Select the Cup size; press the Specialty Brew button.
4. When brew is complete, stir to combine.

**Size:** Cup
**Brew:** Specialty
**Makes:** 1 (16-ounce) serving

# Iced Caramel Macchiato ⓢ

## INGREDIENTS

3 Ninja® Single-Serve Scoops (or 3 tablespoons) ground coffee

2 cups ice

2 tablespoons caramel syrup

¾ cup whole milk

## DIRECTIONS

1. Place the coffee into the brew basket.
2. Place the ice, caramel syrup, and milk into a large plastic cup and set in place to brew.
3. Select the Cup size; press the Specialty Brew button.
5. When brew is complete, stir to combine.

"This is the most delicious version of this classic recipe."

*Sofia*

**Size:** Travel Mug setting
**Brew:** Specialty
**Makes:** 1 (16-ounce) servings

SPECIALTY BREW
(CONCENTRATED COFFEE)

# Iced Cardamom Vanilla Latte

## INGREDIENTS

4 Ninja® Single-Serve Scoops (or 4 tablespoons) ground coffee

½ teaspoon ground cardamom

2 cups ice

¾ cup 2% milk

2 tablespoons vanilla syrup

## DIRECTIONS

1. Following the measurements above, place the ground coffee and cardamom into the brew basket.
2. Place the ice, milk, and vanilla syrup into a large plastic cup; set cup in place to brew.
3. Select the Travel Mug size; press the Specialty Brew button.
4. When brew is complete, stir to combine.

**Size:** Travel Mug setting
**Brew:** Specialty
**Makes:** 1 (16-ounce) servings

SPECIALTY BREW
(CONCENTRATED COFFEE)

# Iced Cinnamon Vanilla Latte

## INGREDIENTS

4 Ninja® Single-Serve Scoops (or 4 tablespoons) ground coffee

½ teaspoon ground cinnamon

2 cups ice

¾ cup 2% milk

2 tablespoons vanilla syrup

## DIRECTIONS

1. Following the measurements above, place the ground coffee and cinnamon into the brew basket.
2. Place the ice, milk, and vanilla syrup into a large plastic cup; set cup in place to brew.
3. Select the Travel Mug size; press the Specialty Brew button.
4. When brew is complete, stir to combine.

**SPECIALTY BREW**
(CONCENTRATED COFFEE)

# Iced Soy Latte

### INGREDIENTS

4 Ninja® Single-Serve Scoops (or 4 tablespoons) ground coffee

2 cups ice

¾ cup soy milk

### DIRECTIONS

1. Following the measurement above, place the ground coffee into the brew basket.

2. Place the ice and soy milk into a large plastic cup; set cup in place to brew.

3. Select the Travel Mug size; press the Specialty Brew button.

4. When brew is complete, stir to combine.

**Size:** Travel Mug setting
**Brew:** Specialty
**Makes:** 1 (16-ounce) serving

# Iced Lavender Latte

## INGREDIENTS

4 Ninja® Single-Serve Scoops (or 4 tablespoons)
ground coffee

1 teaspoon dried lavender

2 cups ice

¾ cup whole milk

2 tablespoons vanilla syrup

## DIRECTIONS

1. Following the measurements above, place the ground coffee and lavender into the brew basket.

2. Place the ice, milk, and vanilla syrup into a large plastic cup; set cup in place to brew.

3. Select the Travel Mug size; press the Specialty Brew button.

4. When brew is complete, stir to combine.

**Size:** Travel Mug setting
**Brew:** Specialty
**Makes:** 1 (16-ounce) serving

# Iced Coconut Milk Latte Ⓢ

## INGREDIENTS

4 Ninja® Single-Serve Scoops (or 4 tablespoons)
ground coffee

2 cups ice

¾ cup coconut milk beverage

2 tablespoons vanilla syrup

## DIRECTIONS

1. Following the measurement above, place the ground coffee into the brew basket.

2. Place the ice, coconut milk, and vanilla syrup into a large plastic cup; set cup in place to brew.

3. Select the Travel Mug size; press the Specialty Brew button.

4. When brew is complete, stir to combine.

**SPECIALTY BREW**
(CONCENTRATED COFFEE)

# Iced Coconut Chai Latte

## INGREDIENTS

4 Ninja® Single-Serve Scoops (or 4 tablespoons) ground coffee

1/2 teaspoon ground cinnamon

1/4 teaspoon ground nutmeg

1/2 teaspoon ground ginger

1/2 teaspoon ground cardamom

2 cups ice

3/4 cup coconut milk beverage

2 tablespoons vanilla syrup

## DIRECTIONS

1. Following the measurements above, stir together the ground coffee and spices; place into the brew basket.

2. Place the ice, coconut milk, and vanilla syrup into a large plastic cup; set cup in place to brew.

3. Select the Travel Mug size; press the Specialty Brew button.

4. When brew is complete, stir to combine.

**Size:** Cup setting
**Brew:** Over Ice
**Makes:** 2 (5-ounce) servings

❄ **OVER ICE BREW**

# Double-Shot White Russian Ⓢ

## INGREDIENTS

3 Ninja® Single-Serve Scoops (or 3 tablespoons) ground coffee

2 cups ice

2 ounces vodka

2 ounces coffee liqueur

4 tablespoons heavy cream

## DIRECTIONS

1. Following the measurement above, place the ground coffee into the brew basket.

2. Place the ice into a plastic or metal cocktail shaker; set shaker in place to brew.

3. Select the Cup size; press the Over Ice Brew button.

4. When brew is complete, add vodka and coffee liqueur and shake well to chill.

5. Divide between 2 glasses, including the ice, and finish each with 2 tablespoons heavy cream.

"The perfect after-dinner drink when you feel like having a cocktail."

Sofia

**Size:** Travel Mug setting
**Brew:** Specialty
**Makes:** 2 (10-ounce) servings

**SPECIALTY BREW**
(CONCENTRATED COFFEE)

# Frozen Mudslide

## INGREDIENTS

4 Ninja® Single-Serve Scoops (or 4 tablespoons) ground coffee

3 cups ice

2 ounces coffee liqueur

2 ounces Irish cream

¼ cup whole milk

2 tablespoons chocolate syrup, plus more for garnish

Whipped cream, for garnish

## DIRECTIONS

1. Following the measurement above, place the ground coffee into the brew basket.

2. Place the ice into a large plastic cup; set cup in place to brew.

3. Select the Travel Mug size; press the Specialty Brew button.

4. When brew is complete, combine coffee and ice with remaining ingredients in a 24-ounce or larger blender container.

5. Blend until smooth, about 25 seconds; divide between 2 glasses and top with whipped cream and chocolate syrup.

**SPECIALTY BREW**
(CONCENTRATED COFFEE)

# Frozen Peppermint Mocha

## INGREDIENTS

4 Ninja® Single-Serve Scoops (or 4 tablespoons) ground coffee

3 cups ice

2 ounces coffee liqueur

1 ounce peppermint schnapps

2 ounces whole milk

2 tablespoons chocolate syrup

## DIRECTIONS

1. Following the measurement above, place the ground coffee into the brew basket.
2. Place the ice into a large plastic cup; set cup in place to brew.
3. Select the Travel Mug size; press the Specialty Brew button.
4. When brew is complete, combine coffee and ice with remaining ingredients in a 24-ounce or larger blender container.
5. Blend until smooth, about 25 seconds; divide between 2 glasses.

**Size:** Travel Mug setting
**Brew:** Over Ice
**Makes:** 4 (4-ounce) servings

❄ **OVER ICE BREW**

# Café Martini

## INGREDIENTS

4 Ninja® Single-Serve Scoops (or 4 tablespoons) ground coffee

2 cups ice

2 ounces coffee liqueur

2 ounces vodka

1 ounce dark crème de cacao

2 ounces Irish cream

## DIRECTIONS

1. Following the measurement above, place the ground coffee into the brew basket.

2. Place the ice into a plastic or metal cocktail shaker; set shaker in place to brew.

3. Select the Travel Mug size; press the Over Ice Brew button.

4. When brew is complete, add remaining ingredients and shake well to chill. Strain and divide between 4 glasses.

**OUR CUPS MEASURE UP.**
The Ninja Hot & Cold Insulated Tumbler has 2-oz. measurement ribs for quick and easy recipe making.

**Size:** Cup setting
**Brew:** Over Ice
**Makes:** 2 (10-ounce) servings

# Coffee Nog

## INGREDIENTS

3 Ninja® Single-Serve Scoops (or 3 tablespoons) ground coffee

2–3 cups ice

¼ cup spiced rum

1 cup prepared eggnog

Ground nutmeg, for garnish

## DIRECTIONS

1. Following the measurement above, place the ground coffee into the brew basket.
2. Place the ice, rum, and egg nog into a plastic or metal cocktail shaker; set shaker in place to brew.
3. Select the Cup size; press the Over Ice Brew button.
4. When brew is complete, shake well to chill.
5. Strain and divide between 2 cups; sprinkle with nutmeg.

"This cocktail is so smooth and delicious!"

*Sofia*

**Size:** Cup setting
**Brew:** Over Ice
**Makes:** 2 (4-ounce) servings

# Almond Chocolate-Kissed Coffee Cocktail Ⓢ

### INGREDIENTS

3 Ninja® Single-Serve Scoops (or 3 tablespoons) ground coffee

2 cups ice

2 tablespoons amaretto

2 tablespoons crème de cacao

Maraschino cherries, for garnish

### DIRECTIONS

1. Following the measurement above, place the ground coffee into the brew basket.

2. Place the ice into a plastic or metal cocktail shaker; set shaker in place to brew.

3. Select the Cup size; Press the Over Ice Brew button.

4. When brew is complete, add amaretto and crème de cacao and shake well to chill.

5. Strain and divide between 2 glasses; garnish with maraschino cherries.

✳ **OVER ICE BREW**

# Coffee Old Fashioned

## INGREDIENTS

4 Ninja® Single-Serve Scoops (or 4 tablespoons) ground coffee

3 cups ice

3 tablespoons bourbon

1 tablespoon crème de cacao

1 tablespoon sugar

4 dashes bitters

2 strips orange zest, for garnish

4 maraschino cherries, for garnish

## DIRECTIONS

1. Following the measurement above, place the ground coffee into the brew basket.

2. Place the ice into a plastic or metal cocktail shaker; set shaker in place to brew.

3. Select the Travel Mug size; Press the Over Ice Brew button.

4. When brew is complete, add bourbon, crème de cacao, sugar, and bitters; shake well to chill.

5. Divide between 2 glasses, including ice, and garnish each with a piece of orange zest and 2 maraschino cherries.

# SWEETS

**NINJA**
COFFEE BAR™

"I love to put this on berries, ice cream, cake, pretty much anything!"

*Sofia*

**Prep time:** 5 minutes
**Cook time:** 7 minutes
**Size:** Travel Mug setting
**Brew:** Specialty
**Makes:** 1 ¼ cups

**SPECIALTY BREW**
(CONCENTRATED COFFEE)

# 7-Minute Coffee Dolce de Leche ⓢ

### INGREDIENTS

4 Ninja® Single-Serve Scoops (or 4 tablespoons) ground coffee

1 can (14 ounces) sweetened condensed milk

### DIRECTIONS

1. Following the measurement above, place the ground coffee into the brew basket.

2. Set a mug in place to brew.

3. Select the Travel Mug size; press the Specialty Brew button.

4. Place sweetened condensed milk in a large microwave-safe bowl, then top with brewed coffee. Whisk to combine.

5. Microwave for 7 minutes.

6. Allow to cool completely, whisk occasionally.

**Prep time:** 5 minutes
**Cook time:** 15 minutes
**Size:** Cup setting
**Brew:** Over Ice
**Makes:** 4 (2-ounce) servings

\* OVER ICE BREW

# Coffee Rum Raisin Sauce for Ice Cream

## INGREDIENTS

3 Ninja® Single-Serve Scoops (or 3 tablespoons) ground coffee

2 tablespoons + ¼ cup dark or spiced rum

¼ cup raisins

1 cup dark brown sugar

1 tablespoon butter

¼ teaspoon salt

4 cups vanilla ice cream, for serving

## DIRECTIONS

1. Following the measurement above, place the ground coffee into the brew basket.

2. Set a mug in place to brew.

3. Select the Cup size; press the Over Ice Brew button.

4. In a small saucepan, combine brewed coffee, 2 tablespoons rum, raisins, and brown sugar, and cook over medium-low heat for 15 minutes.

5. Remove sauce from heat and stir in remaining rum, butter, and salt.

6. Divide ice cream into 4 bowls and top with prepared sauce.

**Prep time:** 15 minutes
**Cook time:** 30–40 minutes
**Size:** Full Carafe setting
**Brew:** Specialty
**Makes:** 1 9-inch layer cake (10–12 servings) and 4 cups frosting

**SPECIALTY BREW**
(CONCENTRATED COFFEE)

# Chocolate Cake with Mocha Buttercream Frosting

## INGREDIENTS

*Cake:*

6 Ninja® Carafe Scoops (or 12 tablespoons) ground coffee

2 cups granulated sugar

1 ³/₄ cups all-purpose flour

2 teaspoons baking soda

1 teaspoon baking powder

1 teaspoon salt

³/₄ cup unsweetened cocoa

2 eggs

1 cup buttermilk (If you don't have buttermilk on hand, combine 1 tablespoon white vinegar with 1 cup milk.)

¹/₂ cup vegetable oil

1 teaspoon vanilla extract

*Frosting:*

2 sticks unsalted butter, room temperature

3 cups confectioners' sugar

1 tablespoon cocoa powder

¹/₄ cup reserved coffee

2 teaspoons vanilla extract

¹/₂ teaspoon salt

## AKE DIRECTIONS

1. Preheat oven to 350°F. Grease and line 2 (9-inch round) baking pans or one 1 (13x9x2-inch) baking pan with parchment paper.

2. Following the measurement above, place the ground coffee into the brew basket.

3. Set the carafe in place to brew.

4. Select the Full Carafe size; press the Specialty Brew button.

5. Set aside 1 cup brewed coffee for the cake, and reserve the remainder for the frosting.

6. Stir together sugar, flour, baking soda, baking powder, and salt in a large bowl.

7. In a large measuring cup, mix together 1 cup brewed coffee and cocoa powder and add to dry ingredients. Then add eggs, buttermilk, oil, and vanilla; beat with a mixer on medium speed for 2 minutes (batter will be thin). Pour batter evenly into prepared pans.

8. Bake 30 to 35 minutes for round pans, 35 to 40 minutes for rectangular pan, or until a wooden toothpick inserted in center of cake comes out clean. Let cool for 10 minutes. Loosen cake from sides of pans, then remove from pans to wire racks. Cool completely.

9. Brush the top of each layer with a bit of coffee, and then frost (see recipe below).

## ROSTING DIRECTIONS

1. Using a mixer with a paddle attachment on medium speed, cream butter for a few minutes. Turn off mixer. Sift confectioners' sugar and cocoa powder into the bowl with the creamed butter. Turn mixer on lowest speed until sugar and cocoa are absorbed by the butter.

2. Increase mixer speed to medium and add ¼ cup coffee, vanilla extract, and salt, and beat for 3 minutes. If frosting needs to be stiffened a bit, add a little more confectioners' sugar.

**Want richer chocolate frosting?**
Add ⅓ cup more cocoa powder to the frosting.

**Prep time:** 5 minutes
**Cook time:** 45–50 minutes
**Size:** Cup setting
**Brew:** Rich
**Makes:** 2 loaves

**RICH BREW**

# Buzzed Banana Bread

## INGREDIENTS

3 Ninja® Single-Serve Scoops (or 3 tablespoons) ground coffee

3 ripe bananas

2 sticks butter, melted

4 large eggs

1 ¾ cups light brown sugar

4 cups all-purpose flour

2 teaspoons salt

½ teaspoon baking soda

1 tablespoon ground cinnamon

½ teaspoon ground nutmeg

1 cup chopped walnuts

## DIRECTIONS

1. Preheat oven to 350°F. Grease and line 2 (5x9-inch) loaf pans with parchment paper.
2. Following the measurement above, place the ground coffee into the brew basket.
3. Set a mug in place to brew.
4. Select the Cup size; press the Rich Brew button.
5. Using a mixer with a paddle attachment on medium speed, mix bananas until mashed, about 3 minutes.
6. Add brewed coffee, melted butter, and eggs. Mix until well combined.
7. In a large bowl, mix together dry ingredients (flour, salt, baking soda, cinnamon, nutmeg, and chopped walnuts).
8. Pour dry ingredients into wet ingredients, and mix on low speed until batter just comes together.
9. Evenly distribute batter into prepared pans and bake 45 to 50 minutes, or until a wooden toothpick inserted in center of cake comes out clean. Cool for 10 minutes before removing bread from pans.

"An affogato is such a classic easy dessert to prepare."

*sofia*

**Prep time:** 5 minutes
**Size:** Travel Mug setting
**Brew:** Specialty
**Makes:** 4 servings

**SPECIALTY BREW**
(CONCENTRATED COFFEE)

# Chocolate Raspberry Affogato ⓢ

### INGREDIENTS

4 Ninja® Single-Serve Scoops (or 4 tablespoons)
chocolate raspberry ground coffee

2 cups vanilla gelato or ice cream

4 tablespoons chocolate syrup

½ cup fresh raspberries, for garnish

### DIRECTIONS

1. Following the measurement above, place the ground coffee into the brew basket.

2. Set a mug in place to brew.

3. Select the Travel Mug size; press the Specialty Brew button.

5. While coffee is brewing, place a 1-cup scoop of gelato each into 4 small cups or ice cream dishes.

6. Divide brewed coffee over the scoops of ice cream in each cup. Top each with 1 tablespoon chocolate syrup, and garnish with raspberries.

**Prep time:** 10 minutes
**Chill time:** 4–24 hours
**Size:** Half Carafe setting
**Brew:** Over Ice
**Makes:** 1 cake (8–10 servings)

# Coffee & Graham Icebox Cake

## INGREDIENTS

3 Ninja® Carafe Scoops (or 6 tablespoons) ground coffee

2 sleeves of cinnamon or honey graham crackers (about 18 whole crackers)

1 quart (4 cups) heavy cream

¼ cup confectioners' sugar

## DIRECTIONS

1. Following the measurement above, place the ground coffee into the brew basket.

2. Set the carafe in place to brew.

3. Select the Half Carafe size; press the Over Ice Brew button. Cool coffee completely.

4. Place ¼ cup cooled brewed coffee, heavy cream, and confectioners' sugar in a large mixing bowl. Beat with an electric mixer on medium speed until soft peaks form.

5. Spread ½ cup coffee whipped cream onto the center of a serving plate. One at a time, brush each graham cracker liberally with some of the remaining coffee, then spread generously with 2 to 3 tablespoons coffee whipped cream. Stack graham crackers one on top of the other to form a cake, then frost with remaining whipped cream on top and sides.

6. Chill in refrigerator 4 to 24 hours. Cut on the diagonal when serving.

"This is one of the best
desserts in the world."

sofia

**Prep time:** 30 minutes
**Cook time:** 4 minutes
**Chill time:** 4-24 hours
**Size:** Half Carafe
**Brew:** Specialty
**Makes:** 8-12 servings

**SPECIALTY BREW**
(CONCENTRATED COFFEE)

# Classic Tiramisu S

## INGREDIENTS

3 Ninja® Carafe Scoops (or 6 tablespoons) ground coffee

6 large egg yolks

1/2 cup granulated sugar

2 cups mascarpone cheese

2 cups heavy whipping cream

1/2 cup coffee liqueur

2 packages (4.7 ounces each) lady finger cookies

1 heaping tablespoon unsweetened cocoa powder, placed in a small sieve or strainer for dusting

## DIRECTIONS

1. Following the measurement above, place the ground coffee into the brew basket.

2. Set a small bowl in place to brew.

3. Select the Half Carafe size; press the Specialty Brew button. Allow coffee to cool.

4. While coffee is cooling, use a double boiler (if you don't have a double boiler, use a small pot full of almost simmering water topped with a large metal bowl). In the double boiler or metal bowl, add egg yolks and sugar, and whisk constantly for 4 minutes, or until egg yolk is light yellow with a smooth, creamy melted marshmallow texture. Remove from heat.

5. Whisk mascarpone cheese into egg yolk mixture.

6. In a separate large bowl, mix heavy cream with 2 tablespoons cooled brewed coffee, then whip until soft peaks form.

7. Add coffee liqueur to remaining brewed coffee.

8. Assemble the tiramisu by dipping lady fingers one at a time into coffee liqueur mixture and placing in an even layer on the bottom of a trifle bowl or ceramic dish. Spread 1/3 of the mascarpone-egg mixture onto lady fingers, followed by 1/3 of the whipped cream, followed by a dusting of cocoa powder. Repeat layers again starting with coffee-dipped lady fingers. The final layer should be whipped cream topped with an even dusting of cocoa powder.

9. Chill in refrigerator 4 to 24 hours before serving.

**Prep time:** 20 minutes
**Cook time:** 15 minutes
**Chill time:** 4–24 hours
**Size:** Travel Mug setting
**Brew:** Specialty
**Makes:** 8 servings

**SPECIALTY BREW**
(CONCENTRATED COFFEE)

# Easy Dreamy Black-Bottom Latte Pie

## INGREDIENTS

50 finely crushed vanilla wafer cookies (about 1 ¾ cups)

3 tablespoons butter, melted

4 ounces dark chocolate, melted

4 Ninja® Single-Serve Scoops (or 4 tablespoons) ground coffee

3 cups whole milk, half & half, or heavy cream

2 packages cook-and-serve vanilla pudding

1 cup heavy cream

1 teaspoon vanilla extract

Ground cinnamon, for garnish

## DIRECTIONS

1. In a medium bowl, mix together cookie crumbs and melted butter, stirring to blend. Firmly press into the bottom of a deep pie plate. Chill for 15 minutes. Brush the melted chocolate over the bottom and up the sides of the crumb crust.

2. Following the measurement above, place the ground coffee into the brew basket.

3. Set a mug in place to brew.

4. Select the Travel Mug size; press the Specialty Brew button.

5. Mix the brewed coffee with 3 cups milk or cream in a 2-quart saucepan. Stir in pudding and cook according to package directions. Cool slightly, then pour into crust. Chill in refrigerator 4 to 24 hours.

6. Whip 1 cup heavy cream with vanilla extract until soft peaks form, then spread over pudding layer. Sprinkle with cinnamon.

**Prep time:** 10 minutes
**Cook time:** 1 hour 20 minutes
**Size:** Travel Mug setting
**Brew:** Over Ice
**Makes:** 1 loaf

❄ OVER ICE BREW

# Marbled Pound Cake

## INGREDIENTS

4 Ninja® Single-Serve Scoops (or 4 tablespoons) ground coffee

2 sticks unsalted butter, room temperature, plus extra for buttering pan

6 ounces cream cheese, room temperature

1 1/2 cups granulated sugar

4 large eggs, room temperature

2 cups all-purpose flour, plus extra for flouring pan

1/2 teaspoon salt

2 tablespoons sour cream

2 teaspoons vanilla extract

1 1/2 cups confectioners' sugar

## DIRECTIONS

1. Preheat oven to 325°F. Butter and flour a 9x5-inch loaf pan, then line the bottom with parchment paper.

2. Following the measurement above, place the ground coffee into the brew basket.

3. Set a mug in place to brew.

4. Select the Travel Mug size; press the Over Ice Brew button. Divide brewed coffee in half and cool.

5. Using an electric mixer with a paddle attachment, cream butter and cream cheese until smooth; add granulated sugar gradually and beat until fluffy.

6. Add eggs, one at a time, beating well after each addition. Add flour and salt all at once, then add sour cream and vanilla extract; mix until just combined. Remove 1 1/2 cups of batter and mix it with half the reserved coffee.

7. Pour half the plain batter into the prepared pan; top with the coffee batter, then the rest of the plain batter. Swirl batter with a knife to create marbling, then tap pan on counter to even out batter.

8. Bake until a wooden toothpick inserted in center of cake comes out clean, about 1 hour 20 minutes. Cool in pan for 10 minutes, then remove from pan and cool completely.

9. Mix remaining coffee with confectioners' sugar to make a glaze. Drizzle over cooled cake.

**Prep time:** 15 minutes
**Cook time:** 40 minutes
**Chill time:** 6–24 hours
**Size:** Half Carafe setting
**Brew:** Over Ice
**Makes:** 1 cake (16 servings)

 ❄ OVER ICE BREW

# Coffee Tres Leche Cake Ⓢ

## INGREDIENTS

3 Ninja® Carafe Scoops (or 6 tablespoons) ground coffee

1 ½ cups flour

1 tablespoon baking powder

4 eggs, yolks and whites separated

1 ½ cups granulated sugar

1 can (14 ounces) sweetened condensed milk

1 can (12 ounces) evaporated milk

1 ¾ cups heavy whipping cream, divided

4 tablespoons coffee liqueur

3 tablespoons orange liqueur

1 teaspoon ground cinnamon

2 tablespoons caramel sauce, for garnish

¼ teaspoon salt, for garnish

## DIRECTIONS

1. Following the measurement above, place the ground coffee into the brew basket.

2. Set the carafe in place to brew.

3. Select the Half Carafe size; press the Over Ice Brew button. Set brewed coffee aside.

4. Preheat oven to 350°F. Grease a 10-inch cake pan and line bottom with greased parchment paper.

5. In a small bowl, combine flour and baking powder; set aside.

6. Using an electric mixer, whip egg whites and sugar on medium-high until semi-stiff peaks form, about 4 minutes.

7. Reduce mixer speed to low; add egg yolks one at a time. Then slowly add flour mixture and ½ cup brewed coffee, alternately, until well combined, about 2 minutes.

8. Pour batter into pan; bake for 40 minutes, or until wooden toothpick inserted in center of cake comes out clean.

9. Allow cake to cool completely, then transfer to a 2-inch deep square casserole dish.

10. Using a fork, poke lots of holes in the cake, making sure to puncture every inch.

11. In a bowl, combine remaining coffee with sweetened condensed milk, evaporated milk, ¾ cup heavy cream, coffee liquor, and orange liquor.

12. Pour mixture over cake, then cover with plastic wrap and chill in refrigerator 6 to 24 hours or until all liquid is absorbed.

13. Whip remaining 1 cup heavy cream with cinnamon until soft peaks form and spread over top of cake. Drizzle with caramel sauce and sprinkle with salt.

**Prep time:** 10 minutes
**Soak time:** 20 minutes–4 hours
**Cook time:** 1 hour
**Size:** Travel Mug setting
**Brew:** Rich
**Makes:** 8–12 servings

RICH BREW

# Toasted Coffee Bread Pudding

## INGREDIENTS

4 Ninja® Single-Serve Scoops (or 4 tablespoons) ground coffee

½ cup raisins

12 cups country white bread, cut in 1-inch cubes (about 16 ounces)

4 tablespoons butter, melted

8 eggs, beaten

1 cup brown sugar

2 ½ cups heavy cream

1 tablespoon vanilla extract

1 teaspoon ground cinnamon

½ teaspoon salt

Confectioners' sugar, for garnish

Heavy cream, for serving

## DIRECTIONS

1. Preheat oven to 350°F. Lightly grease a 13x9-inch glass baking dish.

2. Following the measurement above, place the ground coffee into the brew basket.

3. Place raisins into a mug. Set mug in place to brew.

4. Select the Travel Mug size; press the Rich Brew button. Set coffee aside and let cool.

6. Place bread cubes onto a baking sheet and toast lightly for 10 to 15 minutes. Transfer lightly toasted bread to prepared baking dish.

7. Whisk together remaining ingredients and pour over bread cubes; allow to soak for at least 20 minutes or up to 4 hours, mixing carefully twice.

8. Bake for 45 minutes or until a wooden toothpick inserted in center of bread pudding comes out clean. Sprinkle with confectioners' sugar and serve warm with a drizzle of heavy cream.

**Prep time:** 10 minutes
**Cook time:** 35–40 minutes
**Size:** Travel Mug setting
**Brew:** Specialty
**Makes:** 16 servings

SPECIALTY BREW
(CONCENTRATED COFFEE)

# Coffee Cinnamon Monkey Bread

## INGREDIENTS

4 Ninja® Single-Serve Scoops (or 4 tablespoons) ground coffee

1 cup granulated sugar

1 1/2 tablespoons ground cinnamon, divided

2 cans refrigerated biscuit dough, pieces separated, cut in small chunks

1 stick butter

1 cup brown sugar

1 teaspoon salt

## DIRECTIONS

1. Preheat oven to 325°F and butter a large, 12-inch fluted pan.
2. Following the measurement above, place the ground coffee into the brew basket.
3. Set a large bowl in place to brew.
4. Select the Travel Mug size; press the Specialty Brew button.
5. In another large bowl, combine granulated sugar and 1 tablespoon cinnamon.
6. Roll biscuit dough chunks around in the bowl of coffee until well coated, making sure they don't stick together. Then place biscuit chunks in sugar mixture and turn to coat.
7. Evenly place coated biscuit chunks into fluted pan.
8. In a small bowl, add butter, brown sugar, 1/2 tablespoon cinnamon, salt, and any remaining coffee from bowl, and microwave for 2 minutes.
9. Top dough with brown sugar/butter mixture and bake 35 to 40 minutes or until brown and puffy.
10. Allow to cool 5 minutes, then flip over carefully into a large dish with raised edges. Serve warm.

**Prep time:** 10 minutes
**Cook time:** 30–35 minutes
**Size:** Travel Mug setting
**Brew:** Specialty
**Makes:** 16 servings

**SPECIALTY BREW**
(CONCENTRATED COFFEE)

# Super-Rich Coffee Brownies

## INGREDIENTS

4 Ninja® Single-Serve Scoops (or 4 tablespoons) ground coffee

2 ½ sticks unsalted butter, melted

2 ¼ cup granulated sugar

2 cups unsweetened Dutch process cocoa powder

1 ½ teaspoons salt

1 ½ cups all-purpose flour

4 large eggs

1 cup chopped pecans

1 cup semi-sweet chocolate chips

## DIRECTIONS

1. Preheat oven to 350°F and line a 13x9-inch non-stick baking pan with parchment paper. Then grease pan with baking spray.

2. Following the measurement above, place the ground coffee into the brew basket.

3. Set a mug in place to brew.

4. Select the Travel Mug size; press the Specialty Brew button.

5. Once coffee is brewed, mix all ingredients together, then spread evenly in pan.

6. Bake for 30 to 35 minutes, or until toothpick inserted in center of brownies comes out clean. Allow to cool completely.

7. Remove brownies from pan and cut into 16 pieces.

**Want more cake-like brownies?**
Add an extra egg and cut chocolate chips by half.

**PAIRING SUGGESTION**
Coffee Cake is the perfect partner for your favorite coffee—whatever that may be.

**Prep time:** 15 minutes
**Cook time:** 1 hour
**Makes:** 1 cake (16 servings)

# Sour Cream Coffee Cake

## INGREDIENTS

*Cake:*

- 2 ½ cups all-purpose flour
- 1 teaspoon baking powder
- 1 teaspoon baking soda
- ½ teaspoon salt
- 1 cup granulated sugar
- 2 sticks butter, cut in pieces
- 1 ½ cup sour cream
- 3 large eggs
- 1 tablespoon vanilla

*Crumb topping:*

- 2 cups roughly chopped pecans
- 1 cup firmly packed light brown sugar
- 1 cup all-purpose flour
- 1 stick butter, melted
- 1 tablespoon cinnamon
- ½ teaspoon salt

## DIRECTIONS

1. Preheat oven to 350°F. Butter a 10-inch tube pan.
2. In a large bowl, mix together all ingredients for the crumb topping; set aside.
3. In a medium bowl, combine flour, baking powder, baking soda, and salt; set aside.
4. Using an electric mixer on low-medium speed, cream granulated sugar and butter until fluffy. Add remaining wet ingredients and mix, scraping down sides of bowl, about 3 minutes (mixture will be chunky).
5. Add dry ingredients and continue to mix until thick batter comes together.
6. Layer ½ inch of batter into tube pan, spreading it gently along the bottom and sides. Sprinkle in half the crumb mixture, then evenly layer the remaining cake batter on top. Top cake with remaining crumb mixture.
7. Bake 1 hour, or until wooden toothpick inserted in center of cake comes out clean. Allow cake to cool completely before removing from pan.

**PAIRING
SUGGESTION**
This cake goes great
with our Iced Cinnamon
Vanilla Latte.
(page 89)

**Prep time:** 10 minutes
**Cook time:** 45 minutes
**Makes:** 1 cake (16 servings)

# Apple Fritter Cake

## INGREDIENTS

½ cup milk

2 cups flour

1 ½ cup granulated sugar

3 tablespoons baking powder

1 tablespoon ground cinnamon

2 teaspoons salt

2 eggs

½ stick butter, melted

2 teaspoons vanilla extract

1 apple, peeled, finely chopped

Confectioners' sugar, for garnish

## DIRECTIONS

1. Preheat oven to 350°F. Heavily oil a 12-inch Bundt pan.

2. Combine all dry ingredients in a bowl, and mix thoroughly.

3. In a separate bowl, combine all wet ingredients and mix thoroughly,

4. Add wet ingredients to dry ingredients and mix until a thick batter forms.

5. Pour batter evenly into prepared pan.

6. Bake 45 minutes, or until toothpick inserted in center of cake comes out clean. Allow to cool, then remove from pan by going around the edges with a knife, then flipping over. Dust with confectioners' sugar.

**Prep time:** 10 minutes
**Cook time:** 25–30 minutes
**Makes:** 12 muffins

**PAIRING SUGGESTION**
Love blueberries? Enjoy these muffins with a Creamy Blueberry Iced Coffee!
(page 30)

# Blueberry Streusel Muffins

## INGREDIENTS

*Muffins:*

2 cups flour

1 teaspoon baking soda

1/4 teaspoon salt

1 stick butter, room temperature

3/4 cup granulated sugar

2 eggs

1 teaspoon vanilla extract

1 cup buttermilk

1 1/2 cups fresh or frozen blueberries

*Streusel topping:*

1 cup flour

1/4 cup granulated sugar

1/2 teaspoon ground cinnamon

6 tablespoons butter, melted

## DIRECTIONS

1. Preheat oven to 350°F. Mix together flour, baking soda, and salt in a bowl; set aside.

2. Using an electric mixer with a paddle attachment, cream the butter. Then add sugar gradually and beat until light and fluffy. Add eggs, one at a time, and then vanilla extract.

3. Alternately add buttermilk and then flour mixture. Mix until smooth. Stir in the berries. Transfer the batter to a muffin-paper lined muffin pan.

4. To make struesel topping, mix together flour, sugar, cinnamon, and melted butter with a wooden spoon. Sprinkle 2 tablespoons of topping over each muffin.

5. Bake 25 to 30 minutes or until a toothpick inserted in the center of a muffin comes out clean. Transfer muffins from pan to a wire rack to cool completely.

**Prep time:** 15 minutes
**Cook time:** 35 minutes
**Makes:** 24 biscotti

# Basic Biscotti

## INGREDIENTS

2 cups all-purpose flour

1/2 teaspoon baking soda

1/2 teaspoon baking powder

1/4 teaspoon salt

1 stick butter, softened

1 cup granulated sugar

2 eggs

1 teaspoon vanilla

1 1/2–2 cups desired flavorings*

Flour, as needed

## DIRECTIONS

1. Preheat oven to 350°F. Grease a cookie sheet with butter; set aside.

2. Sift together flour, baking soda, baking powder, and salt; set aside.

3. Using an electric mixer, cream butter and sugar, then mix in eggs and vanilla. Add flour and desired flavorings* and mix to create dough.

4. Turn dough onto a lightly floured surface and divide into two equal portions. With lightly floured hands, roll dough to create a 12-inch long log and place on a prepared cookie sheet. Repeat with remaining dough.

5. Bake 25 minutes or until golden brown. Remove from oven and let cool 10 minutes.

6. Cut log diagonally into 1-inch cookies (12 per log). Place biscotti base-side down on the cookie sheet and bake for 10 to 12 more minutes. Cool biscotti and place in a cookie tin. Biscotti can be stored for up to 1 week at room temperature or frozen for 2 to 3 months..

*Flavoring Options:
**Almond Anise:** Add 2 cups toasted chopped almonds and 1 teaspoon anise seed.
**Orange Hazelnut:** Add 2 cups toasted chopped hazelnuts and 1 tablespoon orange zest.
**Chocolate Hazelnut:** Add 2 cups toasted chopped hazelnuts and 3 ounces melted chocolate.
**Cranberry, Lime, and Pistachio:** Add 1 tablespoon lime zest, 1/2 cup shelled pistachios, and 1/2 cup dried cranberries.

**Prep time:** 10 minutes
**Cook time:** 17 minutes
**Makes:** 8 scones

# Maple Pecan Scones

## INGREDIENTS

2 cups all-purpose or bread flour

1/4 cup granulated sugar

1 teaspoon baking powder

1/4 teaspoon baking soda

1/4 teaspoon salt

1 stick unsalted butter, very cold, cut in small cubes

1 1/4 cups chopped pecans, divided

1/2 cup sour cream

1/2 cup maple syrup, divided

1 large egg

1 cup confectioners' sugar

## DIRECTIONS

1. Preheat oven to 400°F.

2. Using an electric mixer with a paddle attachment, mix flour, granulated sugar, baking powder, baking soda, and salt.

3. Add butter and mix on low until it is well incorporated and pea-sized, about 2 minutes.

4. Add 1 cup pecans, sour cream, 1/4 cup maple syrup, and egg and mix just until dough forms, about 30 seconds.

5. Form dough into a ball, then place on a non-stick or lightly floured surface. Smash dough down with fingers to create a 7-inch disk. Then cut disk into 8 equal pieces.

6. Place scones on a non-stick baking sheet, and bake for 15 to 17 minutes, or until bottom edges are golden. Cool completely.

7. Stir together remaining 1/4 cup maple syrup with confectioners' sugar to form a glaze. Drizzle scones with glaze and sprinkle with remaining 1/4 cup pecans.

**PAIRING SUGGESTION**
Delight your guests when you serve these scones with our Maple Pecan Coffee. (page 24)

**PAIRING
SUGGESTION**
Enjoy these Lemon Bars
with a hot Cardamom
Vanilla Latte.
(page 54)

**Prep time:** 20 minutes
**Cook time:** 30–35 minutes
**Makes:** 12 servings

# Lemon Bars

## INGREDIENTS

2 sticks unsalted butter, softened

2 cups granulated sugar, divided

2 1/3 cups all-purpose flour, divided

4 large eggs

2/3 cup freshly squeezed lemon juice

Confectioners' sugar, for dusting

## DIRECTIONS

1. Preheat oven to 350°F.

2. Place butter, 1/2 cup granulated sugar, and 2 cups flour into the bowl of a food processor fitted with a dough blade. Pulse until dough just comes together.

3. Press dough into the bottom of an ungreased 9x13 baking dish. Bake for 15 minutes or until firm and golden in color. Cool for 10 minutes.

4. Clean the food processor bowl, then add remaining granulated sugar, remaining flour, eggs, and lemon juice. Process until smooth.

5. Pour lemon mixture over par-baked crust. Bake 20 to 25 minutes. Lemon bars will be soft after baking but will firm as they cool.

6. Cool completely, then dust with confectioners' sugar.

**PAIRING
SUGGESTION**
Enjoy these cookies
with a delicious
Café au Lait.
(page 46)

**Prep time:** 10 minutes
**Cook time:** 12 minutes
**Makes:** 12 large or 24 small cookies

# Salty Chocolate Chunk Cookies

## INGREDIENTS

1 ½ cups all-purpose flour

1 teaspoon baking powder

¼ teaspoon baking soda

2 teaspoons salt

1 stick butter, room temperature

1 cup packed dark brown sugar

½ cup granulated sugar

2 eggs

2 teaspoons vanilla extract

8 ounces bittersweet chocolate, cut in small chunks

1 cup chopped walnuts

Large-crystal sea salt, for garnish

## DIRECTIONS

1. Preheat oven to 375°F. Lightly grease 2 large cookie sheets.

2. In a small bowl, combine flour, baking powder, baking soda, and salt; set aside.

3. Using an electric mixer with a paddle attachment, cream butter, brown sugar, and granulated sugar until light and fluffy. Add eggs and vanilla, and mix until combined. Add flour mixture and mix just until dough forms.

4. Mix in chocolate chunks and walnuts until well incorporated.

5. Scoop out 12 large (or 24 small) heaps of dough onto prepared cookie sheets, spacing them at least 2 inches apart. Flatten down slightly.

6. Sprinkle cookies with large-crystal sea salt, then bake 12 minutes or until edges are golden brown. Allow cookies to cool slightly before moving to wire racks to cool completely.

# INDEX

| | |
|---|---|
| Iced Caramel Macchiato | 88 |
| Iced Cardamom Vanilla Latte | 89 |
| Iced Cinnamon Vanilla Latte | 89 |
| Iced Coconut Chai Latte | 92 |
| Iced Coconut Milk Latte | 91 |
| Iced Lavender Latte | 91 |
| Iced Mocha Latte | 87 |
| Iced Soy Latte | 90 |
| Iced Vanilla Latte | 87 |
| Irish Coffee | 57 |
| Marshmallow Mint Latte | 50 |
| Mocha Latte | 44 |
| Mocha Ninjaccino | 75 |
| Pecan Praline Ninjaccino | 78 |
| Pumpkin Spice Latte | 49 |
| Silk Road Coffee | 56 |
| Sweet Sofiaccino | 76 |
| Vanilla Latte | 45 |
| White Chocolate Hazelnut Latte | 51 |

## SWEETS

| | |
|---|---|
| 7-minute Coffee Dulce De Leche | 104 |
| Apple Fritter Cake | 124 |
| Basic Biscotti | 128 |
| Blueberry Streusel Muffins | 126 |
| Buzzed Banana Bread | 108 |
| Chocolate Cake with Mocha Buttercream Frosting | 106 |
| Chocolate Raspberry Affogato | 110 |
| Classic Tiramisu | 114 |
| Coffee & Graham Icebox Cake | 112 |
| Coffee Cinnamon Monkey Bread | 120 |
| Coffee Rum Raisin Sauce for Ice Cream | 105 |
| Coffee Tres Leche Cake | 118 |
| Easy Dreamy Black-Bottom Latte Pie | 116 |

| | |
|---|---|
| Lemon Bars | 130 |
| Maple Pecan Scones | 129 |
| Marbled Pound Cake | 117 |
| Salty Chocolate Chunk Cookies | 132 |
| Super-Rich Coffee Brownies | 121 |
| Sour Cream Coffee Cake | 122 |
| Toasted Coffee Bread Pudding | 119 |

# NOTES